CREATING CHARACTERS:
How to Build Story People

ABOUT THE AUTHOR

The late Dwight V. Swain focused his life on writing. This took him into newspaper work, magazine staff jobs, pulp fiction, informational film — even chasing guerrillas through Central America as a foreign correspondent.

He taught in the University of Oklahoma's Professional Writing Program for more than twenty years and was honored with the Governor's Arts in Education Award. His books include *Techniques of the Selling Writer*, *Film Scriptwriting: A Practical Manual*, and *Scripting for Video and Audiovisual Media*.

CREATING CHARACTERS: How to Build Story People

Dwight V. Swain

WRITER'S DIGEST BOOKS

Cincinnati, Ohio

Other fine Writer's Digest Books are available from your local bookstore or direct from the publisher.

Visit our Web site at www.writersdigest.com for information on more resources for writers.

To receive a free weekly E-mail newsletter delivering tips and updates about writing and about Writer's Digest products, send an E-mail with the message "Subscribe Newsletter" to newsletter-request@writersdigest.com or register directly at our Web site at www.writers digest.com.

02 01   7 6 5

Library of Congress Cataloging-in-Publication Data

Swain, Dwight V.
    Creating characters : how to build story people / Dwight V. Swain. — 1st ed.
        p.   cm.
    Includes bibliographical references and index.
    ISBN 0-89879-662-8
    1. Fiction—Technique. 2. Characters and characteristics.
I. Title.
PN3383.C4S9   1990
808.3—dc20   90-39640
                                                                              CIP

Edited by Nan Dibble
Designed by Carol Buchanan

For Phyllis A. Whitney . . .
fine writer and good friend

CONTENTS

Preface

PREFACE

Fiction grows from story people.

This book is designed to help you bring such people into being. From it you'll learn barn-brush characterization. Subtlety you'll have to master on your own.

(Remember what Somerset Maugham said about that? "I was surprised when a friend of mine told me he was going over a story he had just finished to put more subtlety into it; I didn't think it my business to suggest that you couldn't be subtle by taking thought. Subtlety is a quality of the mind, and if you have it you show it because you can't help it.")

Why will you learn barn-brush characterization? Because I learned my basics in the action pulps, that's why. Anything else is after the fact.

Beyond that, barn-brush handling is what you need to start. It focuses you on the basics and it's easy for both reader and writer to understand.

Not that you'll stop there, please note. Indeed, you *can't* stop, because with every story you write your mind will automatically reach out, groping for better, more effective ways to draw your people. As you find them, make them part of your private kit of literary tools—your skill will increase and your work will improve in keeping with your taste and the direction of your aspirations.

So, here we'll start with the broad strokes of a barn brush, and don't be disdainful of the techniques this approach offers. It works, believe me. Indeed, if you're of an analytic turn of mind, you'll soon discover that, each in his or her own way, the men and women who created the world's classics used the same devices presented here.

How should you use this book? A good way to start, it seems to me, is a quick scan. That will give you an idea of your present skill, and where you're strong and weak. Then you can decide for yourself what's old and what's new—to you, that is—and where you need to dig in and bear down.

I do *not* suggest that you work by the numbers, as it were. That's a sure way to make writing a drudgery, and writing's hard enough without that. Rather, fly by the seat of your pants, setting down characters as they surface in your story. Then, go back and troubleshoot the product, reworking to improve any of your people whom you feel might benefit.

The key word above, please note, is *improve*. Anyone can create a character. What I offer here are merely some time-tried devices by which to make such pseudo-beings better. Sometimes. Because even the best of devices won't always work. At its heart, ever and always, writing remains—to a greater degree than we like to admit—a trial and error process. So as you work and study to acquire skill, never forget to pray a little too, for in the clinch we all need to have Lady Luck riding high upon our shoulders.

It's the custom in a book like this for the author to acknowledge the help he's received from others along the way.

For me, the list would be far too long to include here—the more so, since memory being as fallible as it is, some not included would be sure to have hurt feelings. Let me say only, therefore, that I've learned about character and characterization from every book I've ever read, every student I've ever taught, every editor who's bought or rejected my work.

One name just can't be left out, however: that of my wife Joye R. Swain, whose keen insights and discerning eye—and whose too-often frayed and raveled patience—helped to give this book its cutting edge.

Words can't express my gratitude to her.

THE CORE OF CHARACTER

*What's the one key element any
major character must have?
The ability to care.*

The core of character, experience tells me, lies in each individual story person's ability to care about something; to feel, implicitly or explicitly, that something is important.

Be aware, please, that it doesn't matter whether this something is major or minor, cataclysmic or trivial, or at any level in between. It may be money that's important to him, or family, or world peace, or ecology, or a vacation, or country living. What matters is that he cares about it.

Additionally, it really is inconsequential whether Individual is aware that he feels the way he does. The crucial issue is that the feeling exists to the point that it's strong enough to move him.

How does this build into a story?

Here is a man—an orderly man, we'll say arbitrarily. He's neat by habit—so much so that he's hardly conscious of it, doesn't even think about it. His shirts are folded neatly in their drawer, his ties hung on a proper rack, the bills in his billfold arranged in order so that the fifties are in the back, the ones in front.

Now he marries. His wife, it proves, is content to let dirty clothes pile up in the corner of the bedroom. The living room floor is ankle deep in junk mail and old newspapers. Dishes go unwashed for two days, three days, a week.

Order is important to Husband, he discovers—far more important than he realized. Or maybe he doesn't discover—that is become aware of—his compulsion to orderliness, save in terms of scowls and sullenness and flaring temper. He forgets all the reasons he married Wife—her charm, her intelligence, her spontaneity, her sense of humor, her laid-back, relaxed way of looking at the world.

All he can think of now is her insouciance where order is concerned.

Do you see what's happening? We started with a stick figure labeled "man." Add something that's important to him, something that he cares about consciously or otherwise — the focus on order — and he becomes a person. A character has begun to take form.

Is this all there is to it? Don't be ridiculous. Character creation is a deep and involved subject, as witness to that you're holding a whole book focused on it. But no matter how far or fast you go, the core is still an individual character's capacity for caring, his ingrained ability to feel that something is important. Once you understand that, you've jumped the highest hurdle in the process of creation.

You need to remember, however, that not all characters have the same potential for building into a story. The freaky, the repellent, the boring are unlikely candidates. Indeed, quite possibly they'll alienate most readers. Your best bets are sympathetic characters — characters with whom the reader is able to share and empathize, at least in imagination. And if we use evil characters, they must intrigue us, even though we can't accept their goals.

That said, let's take the story/character building process a step further. How do you make a character feel that something's important?

As a writer, it's alleged that you're creative. So, faced with conceiving a character, you devise — spell that "think up" — an idea or approach that appeals to you. That is, you ask yourself, "How do I bring this lump of mud to useful life? How do I turn him on so he'll move through my story like a reasonable, believable human being?"

The answer to those questions, nailed down as specifically as I know how, is: You assign him an element about which he can care, a factor that looms important to him. You make him a boy with bad eyes; he can't play baseball in a school that lives and breathes the game, and that makes his tape collection the most vital thing in the world to him. Or she's a girl who aches so badly for the father she never knew that she'd sell her soul for kind words from an older man.

You do this flat-footedly. Why? Because you're the boss, the writer. You know what you need, so you brush aside the temptation to vaporings and the permissive, and approach Character on the same level that a housewife stirs up a cake or a brick mason mixes cement. It's no time for whims and fancies. There'll be opportunity and then some for them later. Right now, what you need is a light to guide you.

When assigning a "caring" element to a character, you commit him to a stance which, implicitly or explicitly, consciously or unconsciously, he automatically will live by. Knowing this is Character's dominant dynamic, you write with more confidence and more assurance. You'll find few tools more valuable.

You fit this to your needs, of course; choose what Character is to find important in keeping with the story you plan.

Then, you figure out ("rationalize" is the dictionary term for it) why Character feels the way he does.

When the time at last comes to write the story, plunge him into a pre-planned situation that challenges the part of him that cares, threatens the thing he feels is important.

You focus and sharpen this to the point that Character just can't stand it, and then chronicle the thrust-and-parry of the challenging element and Character's reactions clear through to the story's ending.

Does this apply on all levels? Test it yourself on whatever literary figure you choose, from Batman to Raskolnikov. And yes, it *is* flexible, adaptable.

Thus, life and the drive to survive being the force that it is, a madman with an axe will get a response from virtually any of us. At the other end of the scale, is dignity the issue? There are those to whom it's so important that ridicule may well loom more threatening than death. Money? Slum children can respond to it in terms of peddling crack, just as the Ivan Boeskys and Robert Vescos react to the same stimulus with financial chicanery and market manipulation. A girl may feel that the disapproval of her boyfriend is a disaster worse than an unwanted pregnancy. Her mother, a fading beauty queen, may try to forget her mirror in a bottle.

Am I oversimplifying? Yes, of course. But we'll explore the ramifications of such dynamics—in people and characters alike—in more detail in later chapters. For the moment, however, be content to know that only the character who cares about something, finds something important, is worth bothering with. Ever and always, caring is the core of character. Without it, you have nothing.

Work to make every man and woman in your story a separate and distinct individual—at least, an *imitation* of an individual. I've frequently (for the sake of clarity) used relatively stereotyped people as examples in this book, but don't let that make you think *all* characters should be this broadly drawn. Competing in the market, you can't afford that kind of thing. Your characters *must* appear to be individuals if you're to succeed.

What we're concerned with here is how to build a character from scratch, not story construction and dynamics. So though there's no such thing as a standard operating procedure or one right way where creating story people is concerned, it's time we explored Chapter 2, "Searching Out Your Characters," which gives a tentative mode of attack on the problem of creation that many writers have found useful.

2

SEARCHING OUT YOUR CHARACTERS

How do you find the right character? You scan the applicants until you locate one who turns you on and fits the part.

Building a character begins with deciding which character to build.

Or, to put it on the practical level, if you need a plumber, you hire a plumber. Maybe you check the classifieds or call the union or look in the yellow pages.

Unfortunately or otherwise, there are no yellow pages in the writing business. Which is the trouble with analogies. They so seldom fit exactly.

So, in practice, how do you create characters?

You start from a foundation of your own fantasies and feelings. Because the character you can't fantasize and feel with will fail.

Back to our plumber analogy. When at last he shows up on your doorstep, you look him over and decide whether you like his looks—whether he impresses you favorably or not. And you probably don't go with the filthy one or the one with booze on his breath or the one that flicks cigar ash all over your prized oriental rug.

In other words, you hunt till you find one whose looks you like . . . one who fits your private standards.

You do just that. You find them. And no, I'm not joking.

Perhaps another analogy will make the point clearer—one that will ring bells of memory with virtually all of us, a practically universal experience, at least for males.

Picture yourself, if you will, as male, aged sixteen or eighteen or twenty, and as lonely for female companionship as only a sixteen- or eighteen- or twenty-year-old man can be.

Now, here comes a girl. Maybe you know her; maybe you

don't. Maybe she's pretty; maybe she isn't. Maybe she's black, maybe she's white, maybe she's Oriental or Hispanic or Amerind or Hottentot. It doesn't matter. Because win, lose, or draw, she simply doesn't turn you on. You couldn't care less if she had a full beard or three heads.

Exit Girl No. 1. Enter Girl No. 2. A blonde, this time, complete with Dolly Parton cleavage, swivel hips, and a sidewise glance that makes words strictly superfluous.

The eyes of the boy next to you go wide. "Hey, will you look at that!"

"*You* look," you shrug. Because Little Miss Swivel-Hips, like Girl No. 1, leaves you cold.

A third girl passes. A fourth. A fifth. And still your pulse stays steady; your temperature just won't soar.

Only then, along about Girl n, something happens. Why, you don't know. Maybe you never will. But all at once there's a quickening of the blood, a feeling you haven't felt before. And it doesn't matter that Buddy makes moaning sounds and mutters, "What a dog!" or calls attention to the pustulant acne or the horn-rimmed glasses or the Hindu caste mark or the wrestling champ escort. Because this time, all that matters is that, somehow, a psychobiological spark has been struck and you know that win, lose, or draw, you want to know Girl n better.

In a word, she plugs into your unconscious fantasies, the images and empathies that swirl through the nether reaches of your mind.

The same principle applies where fictional characters, story people, are concerned. One after another, you sort through their assorted possibilities hunting for one who turns you on — which is to say, fits your private quirks and standards — where the particular role you're casting is concerned.

This business of finding characters who turn you on is important on a variety of levels. Not the least of these, often overlooked, is the fact that when you begin any fiction project, you're committing yourself to living with the story people involved for what may develop into a considerable period of time. The classic example is Sir Arthur Conan Doyle and Sherlock Holmes. Doyle eventually became so weary of writing about Holmes that he killed him off in the famous scene at the Reichenbach Falls — and then, to placate outraged readers, was forced to bring him back to life again for endless further stories.

With that in mind, you can see how vital it is not to trap yourself into working with a character you find drab or boring or tiresome. Even a short story can drag on interminably if your protagonist—or any other major player, for that matter—puts you to sleep. So keep on with your searching and shuffling until you spotlight someone who both fits your story's requirements and excites you.

You may be surprised at that person. Once, for me, it was a dragon-riding warrior with blue skin. On another occasion a Cretan princess, Ariadne, caught my private spotlight. Same for a crippled World War II veteran named Tomczik; and an Indonesian Dutch girl, Anita Van Pelt of Djaimaling; and Mr. Devereaux, a footloose gambler in the pioneer West. For mystery writer Lawrence Block there was a man who couldn't sleep; for Tony Hillerman, his Navajo neighbors in New Mexico. John D. MacDonald came up with a "knight in slightly tarnished armor" named Travis McGee who lived aboard a Florida houseboat called the *Busted Flush.* Victor Hugo found fascination in a hunchback, Quasimodo. Shakespeare won immortality with such diverse figures as Hamlet, Juliet, Falstaff, and Lady Macbeth—she of the bloodstained hands.

Now the point of all this is that, actually, "finding" a character means personifying—that is, giving human form to—aspects of yourself that you like, or dislike, or wish you had. For at root we're all writing about ourselves. Or, to put it even more pointedly, all your characters are you.

A conscious process? Seldom. Most of us don't know ourselves that well. But we do, in the phrase, "know what I like." When, for whatever reason, a flash of excitement strikes us as we grope for a character on which to hang our current project, we recognize it—which is to say, it stirs and rouses us to some degree or other, thus encouraging us to explore it further and, if that stimulates us even more, to develop it in greater depth. Tarzan was born this way, I have a feeling. So were Moll Flanders, and Oliver Twist, and D'Artagnan, and James Bond, and Scarlett O'Hara, and Dr. Fu Manchu. Such story people come into being only if they fascinate Writer as well as Reader.

IMPROVING YOUR PERFORMANCE

Can you improve your performance in this area—increase your flash-of-excitement ratio?

Indeed you can. The trick is to explore your own reactions until

you find what stimulates them most. Music often proves effective —
I created any number of science fiction people to the dark strains
of Bartok's Concerto for Orchestra.

The company of particular people can help, too. So can the
right — for you — reading matter. I have a horror-*aficionado* friend
who finds endless inspiration in an old Charles Addams book, *Dear
Dead Days*. A woman romance specialist of my acquaintance
wouldn't miss the lonely hearts columns for the world. The photos
in the movie magazines and the *Academy Players Directory* are cher-
ished by many a writer, and there are clinical psychologists who
swear by the much-debated Szondi Test, with its pictures of Euro-
pean psychiatric patients, as a means of probing their clients' psy-
ches.

Whatever your approach, the important thing is to let yourself
go, via free association and sans self-censorship. For as the late
Howard Rodman, a superior TV writer, once commented, "A
writer must not be judgmental. Look at people and love them, good
and bad, interesting and dull. Cherish them, for they are the stuff
of which your writing will be made."

How do you adapt the characters you zero in on to your story?

Alfred Hitchcock put it well: "First you decide what the characters are going to do, and then you provide them with enough characteristics to make it seem plausible that they should do it."

In a word, you *rationalize* their presence and behavior.

Regrettably — and, too often, disastrously — many beginning
writers fail to realize this. Shaped by the pseudo-profundities of
academics, analysts, and critics, they have been conditioned to believe that characters are, in effect, real people, who exist independ-
ently of the situation.

Of course, story people *aren't* real. They exist only in the
writer's head. (Which isn't to say that they may not become so real
to him, in the course of his imaginings, that he tends to think of
them as actual living, breathing human beings.)

This being the case, the writer's job where characters are concerned is to create (spell that "dream up") story people whom he
can comfortably make behave in an interesting manner and do interesting things in situations, circumstances, or contexts readers
find interesting — yet at the same time keep the story credible and
the story people believable.

Part of this is pretty much mechanical, of course. We'll take it up in detail later. But the heart of character building is a good deal more involved and subtle. It centers on the writer's ability to figure out *why* the character thinks and does the things he does.

To attach a previously mentioned word to this ability, the writer *rationalizes* the character's behavior.

What is rationalization?

Rationalize: *to provide plausible (but not necessarily true) reasons for conduct. To attribute (one's actions) to rational and creditable motives without analysis of the true and especially unconscious motives.*

You'll probably understand this better if you know how I came to my present way of thinking.

My professional involvement with writing began as a young reporter, covering everything from police to garden parties, city hall to civic clubs.

After a few years, that palled. I began to write fiction, and characters came to be an issue. Where did they come from? What shaped their fantasies, their foibles, their thinking? How did you motivate them believably? And so on.

Well, finding them was no problem. My years as a reporter had taken care of that . . .

Item: The aging, small-time storekeeper whose illegitimate son was a world-famous surgeon.

Item: The allegedly happy, married man in his early thirties whom the police knew as a peeping Tom.

Item: The dowdy housewife who had been a gangster's moll.
. . . not to mention the fashionable kleptomaniac, the drunken banker, the transvestite executive, and all the rest.

I knew better than to use any of these estimable ladies and gentlemen *in toto,* you understand. That way lies disaster, in terms of legal action for everything from libel to invasion of privacy to advanced mopery.

Besides, real people will never meet all your story needs. You must adapt them to fit the picture you're trying to create. But it's no chore to combine them in bits and pieces—the hair from one, another's waistline, an eye-cast or lisp or pride or prejudice or sniffle from a third.

The problem is, what made these real people tick? Certainly

you couldn't tell by looking, because each and every one of them wore a mask. Often, it was questionable if even they themselves knew. And when I asked three respected psychotherapists what motivated these people, I got three different answers.

At that point, a fascinating fact dawned on me: As regards what made my people tick, *no one knew.* No one could say for even halfway sure what went on behind those masks—not even the people wearing the masks. When Joe attributed his sticky fingers to childhood poverty, or Hannah said her promiscuity dated back to seduction by an uncle at age eight, or Dr. Carlson argued that Sam exposed himself to little girls because of deep-seated feelings of insecurity where adult women were concerned, each was simply rationalizing—making up a plausible, semi-logical, but not necessarily true explanation for aberrant behavior.

This was equally true for the Reverend Mr. Dunbar, who claimed he'd seen an angel in a vision, and Tom Resnick, whose fidelity to his wife was well-nigh legendary, and Susan Garland, who spent her Sundays visiting the sick and lonely.

Not that any of these people's beliefs, estimable or otherwise, were necessarily wrong, you understand; quite possibly they were right on target. It's just that there was no way, no way whatever, that you could prove or disprove them. Indeed, it was entirely possible to advance other, equally plausible hypotheses to account for each individual's behavior. The Behaviorists could give you one interpretation, the Freudians another, and the Evangelicals yet a third.

Which in turn meant that, for me as a fiction writer, character conception and development took on an entirely new and different twist than I'd originally expected. Specifically, it meant that, within the bounds of my imagination, I was free to create any kind of character I wished, and have him do anything I might conceive, *provided only that I rationalized the character's behavior in such a manner that readers believed it.*

What goes into rationalization? Perhaps another example from my newspaper days will help to clarify the process.

I was interviewing a particularly cold-blooded murderess in jail that day. Finally the session was over. Thanking Murderess, I got up to go.

"That's OK," she shrugged. "But ain't it hell we had to meet in here?" Her gesture summed up the cell's vomit-green walls, the bars, the strap-iron cot. "What a hell of a party we could have had if we'd been outside!"

Her words sent a chill through me. I mean, my psyche was terrified. Because in that moment I found pictures flashing through my head of how a trusting boyfriend, dancing with her, had died.

More to the point, it dawned on me how completely she and I lived in two different worlds.

That matter of private worlds — it's a subject to which I've given a lot of thought in the years since then. From it, increasingly, I've gained insight into what a writer does . . . the difference between the storyteller and other people.

Specifically, in the act of thinking through a story, the writer temporarily suspends his own standards and adopts those of someone else. That's what a writer does when he creates a character. Because he's in the character-creation business, he must learn to put his own beliefs and attitudes in limbo temporarily and adopt those of someone else: the person about whom he's writing, the character he's creating.

Or, if you want to put it in the bluntest possible terms, he must become a hypocrite, a person who pretends to personal qualities or principles not actually possessed.

LIVING IN PRIVATE WORLDS

That's what I'd done where Murderess was concerned. For the sake of insight and a good story, I'd tried to put myself in her place, pretended to see her situation through her eyes. And I'd done it convincingly enough that she'd assumed we were on the same wavelength to a degree that, under different circumstances, might have led to parties.

Such affectation of empathy isn't limited to writers, of course. Actors share it with us, and so do lawyers and con men and spies and undercover police agents and really successful salesmen. The writer who's unable to simulate it faces an almost impossible task, for certainly his characters ever and always will lack the breath of life.

And there's the heart of the matter. Consciously or unconsciously, by nature or by learning, the writer must have or acquire the ability to put himself in another, perhaps unlikely person's place. Sometimes empathy will come in a flash, through intuition or osmosis. A character may spring into being full blown, alive and breathing from the moment of conception. More often, in whole or in part, he and his situation will have to be constructed, fabricated . . . built in steps or stitches through the writer's skill at rationalization. But whatever the process, it remains at the heart of the matter.

Do you see the implications of such thinking? Simple and obvious though it be, it provided me with a map for any road I wished to travel . . . gave me a key to unlock the secrets, thinking, and mysteries of any and all story people.

Beyond this, character is also inextricably linked to context. Separated from situation, it becomes meaningless. Sans puzzles to solve, Sherlock Holmes fades to a shadow figure and holds little interest. Patty Hearst minus the Symbionese Liberation Army is hardly memorable, and neither is Moses unchallenged by an enslaving Egypt, Romeo and Juliet cut loose from the feud between Montagues and Capulets, Captain Queeg apart from the *Caine*, or Hercules without his Labors.

Your unconscious knows this. In consequence, and whether you will it or not, it sees each character that flashes by within the framework of a circumstance, a situation. Instinctively, it conceives and measures your story people against the demands made by particular roles and functions. Out of hand, it rejects the dullard, the weakling, the distasteful—unless that kind of person is what the story demands, or unless some quirk that can give them life and color has caught your fancy.

That being the case, in all likelihood you'll find that automatically, spontaneously, you'll conceive your people in context.

It will help you in all of this if you'll teach yourself to think in terms of your own likes and dislikes. These are always your basic raw material when it comes to character construction. In the manner of a "method" actor, search your past for memories vibrant with emotion—experiences that still have the power to stir your blood, quicken your breathing. Now is the time to make those moments of pain, rapture, and humiliation pay off. What spurred them in the first place? What made you cringe, or catch your breath, or burn with shame to the very roots of your hair?

Why? Because these *reactions* are something you share with the whole human race—not the experiences that evoked them necessarily, you understand. Your agonies of grief may reflect a puppy you lost in childhood rather than the anguish of a husband as the clods thud on his dead wife's coffin. The rage that still knots your belly, when you let yourself think about it, is quite possibly the product of a girl's casually contemptuous laugh, not the frenzy of being falsely accused of treason or the fury of seeing your daughter's murderer go free.

What counts, then, is that you *feel*—and feeling makes you kin to all mankind.

It also links you to your story people. It's the core of character we talked about in Chapter 1.

This fact was driven home to me by the experience a friend of mine had a few years ago. It involved a lady named Clarice.

Clarice's trade was pornography. She was a writer of what in the trade were known as "docs"—pseudo-sociological paperbacks that pretended to be scholarly and factual and that bore titles like *Aggression, Repression and Rape, Secretaries and Sex,* and *The Lesbian Housewife*—that kind of thing.

At the moment, Clarice had an idea for what she swore would prove an all-time best seller. But she felt she needed a collaborator, and my friend was elected.

Her idea? To produce what she referred to as a "turn-on" book.

"Everyone in this world is trying to score," she explained. "Trouble is, they don't know how. The men can't figure out what turns women on, what turns them off. Vice versa for the women. So they jump the track, make wrong moves, do things that upset the apple cart."

"So where do I come in?" Friend asked.

"Isn't that obvious?" Clarice patted him on the knee. "Kelsey, you're all the men in the world. I'm all the women. So, you spell out what women do that turns you on, what turns you off. I do the same for men. So what if we aren't one hundred percent on target? We'll hit often enough that the customers will more than get their money's worth."

Well, they never did get around to writing the book. But Clarice's logic, the principle on which her turn-on book was to be based, remains sound: Certain aspects of human behavior rate positive with the vast majority of members of our culture. Others come through as negative. So if you set up your characters with these in view, you'll improve your odds in favor of winning favorable reader reaction.

In practical terms, this means your first step towards creating an effective character is to look around for people who rouse strong feelings in you. People you admire, one way or another. People you like. People that bother you or baffle you or that you detest. People who intrigue you. People you envy, or with whom you'd like to trade places—not just in terms of situation or status, but of attributes.

Your next step is to ask yourself, considering the kind of story you want to write, might any of these people, these attributes, fit in? Is there a woman you wish you knew? A man who has the qualities—unlikely qualities, quite likely—that might fit a different hero? Can you conceive a unique villain, or band of villains—remember the Alec Guinness film, *The Lavender Hill Mob*, or Jack Bickham's *The Over-the-Hill Gang*?

None of these may strike a note, you understand. I never said writing was easy. But at least now you know what you're looking for: the character who turns you on, excites you. And yes, you'll find that character, if you keep hunting.

Whereupon, you'll move on to Character No. 2. A compatible character, of course, one who fits in with Character No. 1 on one level or another.

And then to Character Nos. 3 and 4 and 5 and any others you may need. And no, quite possibly you won't do them one by one as I have here. You play it by ear, juggling and manipulating and balancing one of your group against another, until you've got a cast that has you so high you just can't wait to work with it.

Not that that's all there is to this business of searching out your characters. Far from it. But it's a start, a first step, and experience will teach you what comes after.

Meanwhile, it's time to move on to another vital matter: How to label each story person so he or she strikes a clear and distinctive note and makes the right first impression on your readers.

We'll take it up in the next chapter.

3

LABELS, LABELS

Why do you label a character?
Your reader needs some clue or
two to help him recognize each
of your story people.

So there's this woman. You were introduced to her at a party a week ago. Now you can't place her.

"Oh, you know!" your wife reminds you. "She was the loud, pushy one. The one who used to be a travel agent."

Indeed, now, you do remember. Because your wife has given Woman *labels*. She has defined Woman as *loud, pushy,* and *travel agent*.

An important step, that, for we live in a world of labels, of identifying designations. One way or another, each of us makes an impression on those around us. Our friends and associates think of us as bumbling or belligerent, active or anemic, crude or crabby. Justly or otherwise, we go through life cataloged as sinner or saint, extrovert or egghead, nice or nasty. Doctors diagnose us as "Type One diabetic" or "Cushingoid" or "hypertensive." Police classify criminals in terms of verbal description (*"portrait parle"*), fingerprints, DNA, *modus operandi* (method of operation in committing crimes). Teachers describe our children as cooperative or withdrawn or disruptive.

Thus it is that Wife has brought Woman into focus for you. Specifically, she has captured and verbalized Woman's *dominant impression* . . . the amalgam of qualities that makes Woman memorable to others.

That matter of dominant impression—few tools are more useful to a writer who seeks to characterize his story people. Four basic elements go into it: *sex, age, vocation,* and *manner*.

The first two of these components might be termed implicit, the second two, explicit.

Item one, sex, is simple enough. Describing anyone, we almost automatically zero in on gender: "this man," "that woman," "he," "she."

Item two, age, gets attention primarily in terms of deviations from an assumed norm of adulthood, as in "little girl," "boy," "old man," "young woman," "teenager," and so on.

The other two constituents, those which I term explicit, operate on a considerably different level.

Item three, vocation, is a noun, a special noun. I call it a *noun of vocation,* because it states the person's occupation — his role in society, what he does for a living. Here we encounter not only the usual range of doctor, lawyer, merchant, chief, and the familiar trades, but also some we may not normally think of in occupational terms — housewife, bum, invalid, bag lady, "significant other." Yet each defines a group and gives dimension to its individual members and so should be thought through and included.

Finally, item four brings us to what I designate as an *adjective of manner* — an element which I firmly believe to be the most important factor in creating a dominant impression.

Manner is, of course, an individual's personal bearing; his or her habitual stance and style. When your wife says a woman is "loud and pushy," she defines her far more sharply for story purposes than any description of blue eyes, blonde hair, or pug nose.

Why? First, because manner is what impresses those who meet Character. More than appearance, ordinarily, you *notice* that a boy is timid, a girl shy, a woman whiny, a man grouchy.

Second, manner indicates to a considerable degree what's going on inside Character. Irascibility of manner is a red flag warning of a potential punch in the nose. The bold-eyed girl isn't likely to be taken aback by a boy's brash come-on. A prospect's air of cringing humility tends to bring gladness to the aggressive salesman's heart.

Test this against your own experience. Isn't Old Max frequently identified as "that clumsy mechanic"? Edna is "the nosy clerk at the Welfare." Lorraine? "Our sympathetic schoolteacher." Tom? "The driver with all the jokes." And Mr. Sloan, the office manager, will live forever as "his moronic majesty."

For the writer, the dominant impression offers yet a third bonus: A character's manner gives you something predictable to write to. You know in advance how he'll tend to behave, so you know the kind of words he's likely to speak and the things he's likely to do.

Note how nicely the noun of vocation fits in with this. Just as situation provides a context for character, occupation gives you a context for manner. Combine the two—sloppy waitress, surly cop, forthright mill hand, friendly druggist, worried nurse—and your people begin to take on at least a semblance of life.

Flexibility in planning comes too. Make the surly cop a sloppy cop or a forthright cop or friendly cop or worried cop, and he becomes a totally new person. Frequently such switches can even be parlayed into intriguing, character-defining, contradictory touches that add extra interest. Let happenstance throw the wise-cracking secretary into contiguity with the long-faced undertaker, and you may find yourself contemplating a twist that gives you a long-faced secretary and a wise-cracking undertaker; and yes, I've known a couple of the latter, even though they generally succeeded in restraining themselves when solacing the bereaved cash customers. The stupid professor, the pompous doctor, the hypocritical clergyman (remember Elmer Gantry?), the pious prostitute—the list could go on and on, and all offer possibilities.

This probably is a good time to bring up a related issue: Is the dominant impression a character gives right or wrong, accurate or inaccurate? If you meet a man dressed in neo-Nazi regalia and with a skinhead shaved scalp, you automatically assume that his beliefs, thinking, and behavior patterns reflect the image. Clerical dress and a Roman collar registers something else again.

The point is that, rightly or wrongly, we do judge by first impressions, and those first impressions are hard to overcome. Present a boy stealing a purse the first time he appears in your story, and your readers will respond, "Of course. He's a thief," when he later is shown burglarizing a gas station. But if the first time you bring him on stage he returns a dropped wad of bills to an elderly woman who doesn't know she's lost it, then later is caught in a robbery, Audience will think, "Hey, that kid's honest. What's happened to make him switch?"

The point is, if you strike one note at the start of a book, changing the picture in your readers' minds so they'll accept that Character was playing a role and had reason for doing so will take careful planning and planting as the story develops.

There are two more questions to consider when creating a character's manner:

Question 1: How do you find the right adjective?

Observation is the answer, of course. For while you've grown up aware of mood and manner, odds are you've never paid them proper heed.

Now's the time to remedy that deficiency. To that end, make it your business to pay attention to the behavior of the people you meet, on every level. Focus on it, labeling manner. Is this man blank-faced or bored or blasé? Is the one next to him uncertain or scared or nervous? Is the woman suspicious or sick or tired? What image is her friend trying to project? Disdain? Superiority? Hauteur?

Question 2: How do you capture manner?

While finding adjectives, putting labels to manners, you also gather incidents that convey impressions — even if later you don't use them. Collect or devise bits which will reveal precisely *why* people think of this person or that as roughneck/roué/saint/sad sack or what have you. What does he *do* that leads others to think of him in such terms? Does he blow his nose on a linen napkin at a formal dinner? Suffer agonies rather than use a public restroom? (Remember Mark Twain's famous comment that modesty had ruined more kidneys than bad liquor?) Push little old ladies aside in order to get a better seat in a theater or bus?

Do I hear cries of outrage? Angry voices protesting that few of us fit into such simplistic packaging? Said voices are right, of course. Simplistic labeling often gives a false impression. I admit it frankly.

What to do about it? The answer, of course, is to *modify* the label — insert *ifs, ands,* and *buts* into the character as needed to flesh him out. But that's a subject calling for attention on a different level. We'll take it up in a later chapter.

Does this mean you introduce each character with his dominant impression? Not necessarily, though it's certainly not the worst way to go.

Indeed, on occasion, you may set down pages without stating the dominant impression a character makes in the specific terms of the vocation/manner pattern I've described. You may, instead, bring him or her on with a memorable or colorful tag — a toupee that's forever slipping down, false teeth that keep getting in the way of speech, or the like. Or use minor action: "A girl opened the door. 'This way, sir,' she said." Or, "The man wriggled through the mud to the fence." That kind of thing. After all, there are all kinds of situations in this life where a person remains virtually faceless and so doesn't make a real impression, plus or minus. What counts is that you get him on stage. Defining him can come later — though not too much later.

You yourself should surely know the dominant impression behind such a mask, simply because you'll need it in order to write about the person effectively later on. Maybe, at the moment, the girl who opens the door above doesn't register. But if she's going to play a part of any consequence later on, it will help if she's a slattern or a flirt, young and timid, or old and perpetually disgruntled.

How do you bring in a character? Here are four possible approaches — not the only four, certainly, but they'll do for starters till you devise techniques of your own you like better:

1. **Description, appearance.**
   "The hair was what you noticed. It was bright orange and stacked on top of her head in what they used to call a beehive."
2. **Action.**
   "The man ducked back into the shadows, one foot scraping on the pavement as if he couldn't lift his leg."
3. **Dialogue.**
   " 'Lookin' for someone?'
   "Eleana turned. A woman was standing in the doorway, an old woman a head shorter than she, with pinched features and squinty eyes. 'Who are you?' she gulped.
   " 'Me? Depends on who *you* are, what you want.' "
4. **Thoughts, introspection.**
   "Edwards pondered, scanning the passersby and trying to define the person called X. A man, surely — or was it? The note really hadn't given any hint."

Meanwhile, the principle for simplistic labeling remains both sound and important. For ease of recognition it can't be beat. Far too many writers create characters who are, at best, gray-neutral confusing, when it's totally unnecessary. In life and in fiction alike, unfairly or not, we *do* identify people by labels aptly slapped on them by their fellows.

That such labels may be wrong, of course, goes almost without saying. Externals are handy indeed, but they may distort or contradict what's going on inside a person . . . Not too often, though, or you'll confuse your readers.

That's an aspect of character that's absolutely essential for any writer to understand. We'll explore it in the next chapter, "Fleshing Out."

4

FLESHING OUT

How do you make a character real? You provide him or her with appropriate tags, traits, and relationships.

Labeling — assigning a story person a dominant impression — is a primary step in character creation.

But a dominant impression alone doesn't go far enough. Leave it at that and Character will end up a stick figure at best — a caricature, not a person. If he's to be of any real use to you, you need to flesh him out, develop the picture of him in more detail, internally and externally, inside and out.

Specifically, you need to give him *tags, traits,* and *relationships.*

Before we go further, however, let's emphasize one point too often forgotten, especially by beginners: People are like tapestries; that is, each is woven of many threads. But some threads are more vivid and visible than others, like strands of red through a gray fabric.

It's also important to remember that making a character too complex will kill him. A good character is a *simulation* of complexity, not the real thing. Fairly clear and simple traits work best. Otherwise the effect will be that given by a "busy" painting, one too cluttered with detail. So while ordinarily you'll want to go beyond the cartoon/caricature level, try not to carry development so far in depth that your people fall over the edge into total confusion. The meaningful character in fiction is the one with a salient feature, or two or three, like the real-life Ayatollah Khomeini, Richard Nixon, or Elvis Presley, with individuality and color added via modifying touches.

Thus, in life, we don't know most of our friends and neighbors in depth. They exist for us mainly in terms of dominant impression plus externals — appearance, speech, mannerisms, attitudes, abilities—plus how we get along with them. (Goals? We'll take that up later.)

With that caveat out of the way, let's get on to consideration of the tools you'll use in fleshing out story people: tags, traits, and relationships.

Tags come first.

A tag is a label, but a limited, specialized label. It identifies a character and helps your readers to distinguish one story person from another. Thus, a name is a tag, and it's important. It should identify him, characterize him, give your reader an idea of the kind of person he is and his role. (Witness the skinny black detective nicknamed "Biafra Baby" in William Caunitz's *Suspects;* the "Biafra" and the starvation in that area ties to his being black and gaunt. Or Inspector Herman Schmidt, known to all as "Herman the German"—the stereotype "German" draws an immediate image in colleagues' and readers' minds.)

Names also characterize by telling of age. Relatively few girls today are "Agatha" or "Althea" or "Sophronia," common enough seventy-five years ago. "Kim" and "Kelly" and "Jessica" appear more often. Men? How many Jedediahs or Ebenezers or Zebulons have you met lately?

Naming a bruiser "Percival" or "Algernon" may be out of line, too. If a name isn't appropriate—well, see what Johnny Cash did with "A Boy Named Sue." The late John D. MacDonald had planned to call his McGee character Dallas, until President Kennedy's assassination. Then, concerned that the city's name would create bad connotations where the character was concerned, he rechristened McGee as Travis.

Just how and when you decide on a name is another matter. You may choose it early in your story's planning stages, or you may still be fussing over it until the final typing. One friend of mine even went so far as to set up interim names designed to keep him reminded of each character's role and attributes—"Mr. Satan," "Miss Tease," "Mrs. Frump," and so on. And Martha Kay Renfroe (M. K. Wren) reports that the name of her half-Nez Perce series detective character "actually is sort of an accident."

"I was choosing my detective's name and got as far as Conan Flagg, but I wanted to give him a middle name. Joseph came to mind for some unknown reason. Probably I just liked the rhythm of Conan Joseph Flagg. Then it occurred to me that it might be interesting if the Joseph was in honor of Chief Joseph, the Nez Perce leader. And it was only then that Conan's physical appearance and life history began to come into sharp focus for me. Call it a 'tag,' but his Nez Perce heritage is what gave him a past and even a face."

In any event, one way or another, Character acquires a name. Beyond this, what other tags does he need?

Broken down into categories, ordinarily we speak of tags of *appearance, ability, speech, mannerism,* and *attitude.*

Appearance means that it might be nice if your readers had at least some idea of what each character looks like. Kojak's lollipop and shaved head are tags. So are Long John Silver's wooden leg and Adolf Hitler's mustache. Anarchist Johann Most's bushy beard provided cartoonists with a tag that labeled radicals up to the present day. "Hulk" and "shrimp" differentiate two men. Any item that strikes a distinctive note will do — a habitual cigar between the teeth, a Fu Manchu mustache, green eyes that seem to glow in the dark, uniquely fine or coarse hair, markedly sloppy or fastidious dress, a missing ear lobe, a drooping eyelid, or whatever. Choose two or three items per major character, probably, since you're going to have to use each several times in order to keep readers reminded that Character isn't the albino, or the one with the limp, or the drooler with the false teeth that clatter.

Here, for example, is a "tiny" grandmother in Dian Curtis Regan's *The Perfect Age,* as she reaches up "one small hand to anchor her stylish hat, which perfectly matched her tailored burgundy suit."

Note, incidentally, that Regan doesn't simply say, "Mrs. Jones had small hands." She brings the tag on *in action* . . . has the character *reach up* the hand to anchor the hat.

Further, the hat itself constitutes a tag, for it's a "stylish" chapeau, which "perfectly matched her tailored burgundy suit." The result is an image of a particular kind of grandmother: physically "tiny," in all likelihood a woman of poise and good taste — a far cry from a frowsy grandmother, or a slatternly grandmother, or a gauche, ill-bred, vulgar grandmother, even though Regan hasn't said so in so many words.

Another older woman — this time, from Pat Murphy's *The Falling Woman:* "I am an old woman. My hair is gray and brown — the color of the limestone monuments raised by the Mayas one thousand years ago. My face has weathered through the years—the sun has carved wrinkles around the eyes, the wind has carved lines. At age fifty-one, I am a troublesome old woman."

A far different woman from the Regan grandmother, right? Here we see not only physical details, but a trait of candor: a character not afraid to report honestly on what she sees in the mirror. Also, she admits her age frankly and recognizes the way her associates often see her—"troublesome." And in her analogy—"the color of the limestone monuments raised by the Mayas one thousand years ago"—establishes her intelligence and the focus of her interests.

Or let William Kienzle describe Father Fred Palmer in *The Rosary Murders:* "[He] was forty-seven years old, going on seventy."

Is this a tag of appearance, or manner, or attitude? It doesn't really matter. Here we see a judgment of one person by another, captured in a phrase. ". . . forty-seven years old, going on seventy" is a tag that says it all, even though more details follow.

Ross Thomas, in *Briarpatch:* "Harold Snow smiled back. It was a sheepish smile, patently false, that somehow went with Snow's long narrow face, which the detective also found to be rather sheeplike, except for those clever coyote eyes." Snow is tagged neatly with a "sheepish smile, patently false," and a "long narrow face." Then, the interpretive detail of "clever coyote eyes" adds dimension to the picture and lets us know that Thomas wants us to feel wariness in regard to the character.

Character's *speech patterns* may also be a matter of some import. Repetitions, for example, may help to identify him: "sir," "laid back," "awesome," "dude." Same for accents (Southern, Western drawl, Boston Irish, Brooklynese), *ad infinitum.* And each occupation has its own cant or jargon, as when a policeman refers to an offender as a "perp" (for perpetrator) or an airline pilot speaks of having his "flaps down."

Be careful, however, of introducing heavy, phonetically spelled dialect. Both readers and editors hate it. Why? Because it tends to confuse and slow the pace. You're better off to avoid it.

A good ear and wide human contacts are the best tools to use to capture speech patterns, perhaps supplemented by such works as the Vance Randolph and George P. Wilson volume, *Down in the Holler,* Ramon Adams's *Western Words,* Eugene Landy's *The Underground Dictionary,* or the like. But more of that later in Chapter 13, "The Things They Say." And remember always that slang or colloquial terms tend to age rapidly, so any volume on the subject may be out of date virtually before it's printed.

The matter of *mannerism* (rubbing the chin, an eye tic, a frown, or raucous laugh) also needs to be considered. Jane Fonda's continual business with cigarettes in *Agnes of God* is a mannerism. So is George Raft's coin-flipping in old gangster movies. Same for the character who doodles as he talks, or bites his lip, or continually smooths his hair, or sneaks glances into mirrors. A neighbor has a habit of "neatening up" his front room by gathering any loose printed matter into piles. (It drives his wife crazy. Newspaper clippings and the like disappear into those piles, never to be seen again. But it's a mannerism, like the others.) One and all, they help not only to identify Character, but to make him human.

Attitude is a matter of behavior patterns — a character's habitual way of reacting to a particular kind of situation. Mary Poppins's eternal cheeriness reflects an attitude, and so does Rambo's macho stance. Racism and sexism are attitudes. Ditto sanctimony or ingrained suspicion or anxiety or discontent. And if it pleases you to develop new and different categories of your own, so much the better. (I'll discuss this in more detail in Chapter 6.)

Closely related to tags is the matter of *ability* or *capacity* . . . the potential for Character to do whatever his role in the story calls for. If, for example, the story requires that he deal with a medical emergency, does he have the ability to do so? How about the skill to make a bomb, style a woman's hair, change a diaper, lay cement blocks, clear a fuel line? Failure to provide Character with the ability to perform as required believably can destroy — or make — a story. Life gives you a host of examples. Look how the initial wimpish image of Bernhard Goetz in the New York subway shooting was changed, for example, when it was revealed that he had had handgun training and in crisis adopted a "combat stance."

How to reveal matters of ability? You as a fiction writer must think ahead and plant within your character the capacity to deal with the demands of your story situation. You'll have to discover the tags or traits that fill the bill. Then, make reference to them later as the story develops.

Perhaps this is also the place to remind you of the importance of *contrast* where tags are concerned. No Ann, Alice, and Agatha in the same story unless for a reason. No two blue-eyed blondes, no matching Indians, no stutterers in tandem. The object of tags, remember, is to help your reader identify, differentiate, distinguish.

It's also important that you decide on each major character's *traits:* his or her habitual modes of response and patterns of behavior.

How you go about attacking this issue is a matter of some disagreement. For example, my late, great colleague in the University of Oklahoma's Professional Writing program, Walter Campbell, an analyst to the core, insisted that traits be divided into four groups: human, typical, social, and individual.

In my own view this is mechanical, artificial, and of little practical value. What counts is that you be aware that people do develop distinctive ways of reacting to life's demands, and that these reaction patterns tend to become habitual.

To this end, you need to ask yourself how you want a given person to behave in a particular kind of situation. Is Character a worrier, a soft touch, a grouch, a freeloader, a bully? Is she cruel, kindly, pious, a hypocrite, selfish, unselfish, honest, honest only when observed, considerate, unaware?

So, you decide. Then thrust Character into situations that will give her the opportunity to show the stuff she's made of *before* a crisis arises, so your readers won't be taken aback when Character behaves the way you need her to.

What about *relationship?* Call it the way we interface with others, our associations with and reactions to the people with whom we deal or come in contact.

Each of those contacts and dealings is different. How do we respond to each of these people? How do we feel about them? And yes, we *do* feel about them and respond to them, each and every one, even if it's only in terms of standing up straighter, watching our grammar, or not making an off-color joke.

For fiction purposes, however, we must consider these relationships a good deal more closely. Those individual connections will determine how our characters act and react, how they respond to things their story associates say and do as your epic progresses.

Your most useful tool in handling the obviously complex issue of relationship in your stories will be habitual people-watching, coupled with reading both fiction and psychology.

It also may help you in this area if you'll bear two principles in mind, each with a proverb out of folk wisdom behind it.

The first: *Like attracts like.*

Second: *Opposites attract.*

Now, obviously, neither of these aphorisms is universally true. But they are sound often enough to prove useful when you don't know how to work through a scene. Is Heroine smitten because she and Hero both are Alabama WASPs and love swimming, tennis, camping, computer graphics, and iris culture? Or is the attraction based on the romantic fascination Hero's inner city street-tough stance holds for sheltered, small-town Heroine?

Another point you need to consider is whether to cast a given character *to* type or *against* type.

To put this in down-to-earth form, consider your friend Alex, an individual whom we'll arbitrarily label with a dominant impression as a *scholarly professor.*

In keeping with this label, and helping to translate it into visual terms, we give Alex stooped shoulders, pale face, a frequently furrowed brow, a tendency to long pauses and staring off blankly into space, and a book always in hand.

In so establishing and describing Alex, we're taking the approach termed casting "to type." That is, we're accepting traditional stereotyping, the kind of patterning that gives us the Irish cop, the dumb blonde, the garrulous oldster.

"Against type" means rejecting that image in favor of a more fresh and original picture — one that makes the character an individual rather than a stick figure.

(Which doesn't mean that characters cast "to type" are necessarily to be avoided. Types have their place, particularly where your minor people are concerned.)

Were we to want to cast Alex "against type," however, we could make him egotistical, belligerently opinionated, full of erudite quotes, scowling and with head thrust forward as he attempts to force his ideas on everyone within earshot. He'd still come through as scholarly — but a different kind of scholarly.

Is this enough to characterize Alex for your readers? Mightn't they appreciate it if you'd sharpen the focus? Perhaps make the picture more graphic?

Take his work, for example. There are professors and professors. Some are more drawn to campus politics than to teaching. Others like to ride the gravy train, sloughing off paper-grading or anything else that sounds like work on graduate assistants. Still others are socializers, or grandstanders, or promoters.

His preoccupations, the interests that absorb him, also play a role. As a scholar, is his area of scholarship the issue? Is he totally engrossed in the sociopathy of juvenile delinquents? The poetry of Allen Ginsberg? The neurology of earthworms? Internal dissension among Shiite Moslems?

Or is his scholarship merely a financial facade, while his real focus is on world peace or real estate or travel? Or collecting coins or pornographic photos or Mayan artifacts? Whatever you choose for him will both help to individualize him and influence his behavior in your story.

His love life is an additional matter to consider. For one thing, does he have one, or is he an asexual loner? Is he a happily married man, or are one-night stands his thing? How about "sequential monogamy"—one woman/wife after another? A fascination with young girls, the Lolita syndrome? Homosexual cruising? Do think about it!

His attitude towards society itself is another constituent. Is he gregarious, everybody's friend, a joiner? Do worthwhile causes attract him? Is he active in his community, his professional group, his political group? If not, why not?

Consider, too, your character's weaknesses. What flaws do you want to show in the course of your story—and yes, Character *does* have them; we all do, and you'll be wise to reveal them, for the "perfect" person tends to disgruntle readers. (My own tendency, incidentally, is to speak of a character as "non-perfect." For whatever obscure reason, to say that somebody has a weakness puts a judgmental label on that person that bothers me.)

A good example of such a "non-perfect" person is Murphy Brown (played by Candice Bergen), a character in a TV situation comedy. Murphy is a top TV newsperson—intelligent, efficient, gorgeous to look at. But she's also a recovering alcoholic, a heavy smoker suffering the agonies of quitting, and so aggressive, opinionated, and jealous of her status that she makes your teeth ache. But because she's so human, viewers love her.

Why give a character flaws and weaknesses? Because they constitute tools you can use to help control reader reaction to a character—to make the reader like or dislike her; accept her or reject her. But more of that in Chapter 7, "The Breath of Life."

And so it goes. All these are factors that influence and individualize a character. Some characters, some stories, call for close attention to these factors. In others, the barest minimum will do. You and your audience are the ones who decide.

Beyond such generalities, there are all sorts of rule-of-thumb devices to help you give dimension to a character. How would her best friend describe her, for example? What would Friend say about her? What would her worst enemy's reaction be? How would she see and rationalize herself? What do people like or dislike about her? Do they admire her, pity her, fear her? Does she feel superior to others? Inferior? Does she see herself as good-humored, honest, hard-working, clever, kind, short-tempered, timid, aggressive, understanding, stingy, generous, or what?

Bear in mind, however, that all such traits are abstract and general. Behavior is concrete and specific. "What does he or she *do?*" that demonstrates any given point is what's important.

To that end, you must devise incidents and specific details that *show* the trait in action. Never just *say* a character is irritating. Make him *do* something recognizably irritating. Telling simply isn't good enough. If you want him to be likable, admirable, courageous, or such, figure out a way to prove it in action; that's what writing's all about.

Also, to a degree, you may use what I term the testimonial technique—that is, let some other character recall or describe succinctly a convincing incident that makes the point.

How far will he go in his efforts to attain a goal? What are his limitations? Will he lie? Steal? Kill? Reject a friend? Betray a loved one? You need to decide, because, for the duration of the story, you're god. "What will he have to do?" you need to ask. "How can I make it believable that he'll do it?" Is his behavior a matter of attitude? Function? Potential?

Where do you get all this material? The answer, I must repeat, even though it grows tedious, is through observation and introspection—a study of living, breathing, human beings in their native habitat, and that includes yourself. Nothing will substitute for watching, on the one hand, and probing your own most secret thoughts, on the other.

This is a subject we'll discuss elsewhere in more detail. But it's important to plant the thought in the back of your head early. Nor will it hurt to make contact with others' observations, others' conclusions, as set down in texts on psychology, sociology, and other aspects of behavior.

Neither should you neglect the work of other fiction writers. Their work offers insight on a wide variety of levels, as witness the traditional wisdom that novelists were the first psychiatrists, and that books like Robert Bloch's *The Scarf* have been reviewed in psychiatric journals.

A final question that sometimes comes up in regard to fleshing out story people is the matter of character dossiers, files that catalog the tags and traits and labels and other characteristics of your cast. To what extent should you develop them and use them?

Later in your career, you may work with a series character — one originated and developed by someone else. Nick Carter is a recent case in point and so is Nancy Drew. A dozen or more writers have written books in these names, on assignment. As you sell more and more material, an editor or publisher may ask you if you'd be interested in doing a book using one of the house's characters.

In that case, the character has already been established, complete with tags, traits, relationships, and background. You receive this information in a statement, a dossier, termed a "bible." The longer the series has been in existence, the more specifically the character has been defined — and the more you as a writer are boxed in. Once the character has been given a wife or a twelve-year-old daughter, you're stuck with them. Same for a finger cut off, a phobia about ghosts, a problem with alcohol. You merely integrate this already existing person into a plot.

But we'll assume you're not doing such a series. Should you work up character dossiers? And if so, how detailed should they be?

Most writers give solemn lip service to them, and I'd be the last to say them nay. But I've noted in my contacts with a fair assortment of my fellows that they give more honor to such catalogs in the telling than the fact.

My own tendency is to reverse the pattern most often recommended. Why? Because I get bored at what too often strikes me as busy work. (I remember one writer on writing who insisted that you should know whether your heroine prefers ice cream or pineapple ice.) I also feel that too many details decided early tend to lock you in and make it harder for you to adapt your character to story needs.

In consequence, instead of starting with a detailed dossier, I make a quick pass at laying out my characters. That means assigning each (tentatively and subject to change if my first notion doesn't work out) an occupation, fragments of physical description, dominant impression, and basic attitudes, plus any color details that come to mind.

(This matter of collecting color details, striking fragments and bits of business, is tremendously important, incidentally. Try to think them up when you need them and your brain will tend, too often, to go blank. Better by far to jot them down as they flash by in odd moments. Later, you'll be glad you did.)

Then I write. And as I write, I find I need things. Character A, for instance, needs to know how to pick a lock, so I give her a bit of background involving time spent years before with a locksmith uncle. Character B is going to have to deliver a baby; I plant references to his training as a paramedic. Character C? Her mother was an amateur gemologist/rockhound, so she can identify semiprecious stones.

All this material goes into a sort of working file—a dossier after the fact—as my story progresses, creating the details of characterization catch-as-catch-can as I go.

Then, when my rough draft is finished, I go back and edit and correct and insert.

This is the moment of truth. I discover that I've accidentally included a Joe and a Jobe in the story, and that all three females are redheads. (My wife once was unkind enough to point out to me that my women always had breasts that "rose and fell too fast.") And I've even discovered that the protagonist's goal really was too weak to carry 40,000 words, and had to go back and do a major patch job.

Would I have avoided these flaws with more detailed planning? In some cases, yes. But not always. You simply can't foresee all the facets of a story's development, and trying to out-guess every turn and twist may hang you up for longer than you think. Nor can you fuss and fidget over each precious line—not if you're being paid by the word the way we were in the old pulp days. What we had to do was get the story down on paper; and that, to my way of thinking, is still what's important. Instruction's vital, true. But in the last analysis, in large measure you learn to write by writing.

Indeed, that's why I've handled this book as I have. The raw material is all here, but I've spread it out so you can pick and choose pieces that you need at the moment or that strike your fancy, rather than trying to force patterns on an entity that, after all, is supposed to be your own creation. So much for fleshing out your characters, giving them physical and psychological dimension. It's also important that you have at least some idea why they're the way they are, what cast them in their present mold. To that end, it's important that you know at least key portions of their background.

It's a topic we'll begin exploring in the next chapter, "The World Within: 1."

5

THE WORLD WITHIN: 1

*How do you motivate a character?
You devise something that he or she must
change in order to win happiness.*

When we talk about the world within a character, at root we're
discussing motive: "A mental force that induces an act; a
determining impulse. Intention; purpose; design," as one
dictionary puts it. It is the spine of any story.

Motive, in fiction, is another name for a *desire for change* on
the part of some character or other.

It works this way:

Happiness is the universal human goal.

*Un*happiness, regrettably, is all too often the human state.

For an individual to move from unhappiness to happiness ordinarily means that some aspect of his or her situation—state of affairs or state of mind—must be changed.

Change may be anything from getting a raise to humiliating an
enemy to experiencing the feeling of youth again.

If the desire for change is so strong as to impel an individual to
do something about it, take action to achieve it, it constitutes a
motive.

Stated thus bluntly and simplistically, the picture is obvious.
Give a character so compulsive a desire to make a given change that
he can't let it be, and you have the basis for a story.

In life, the issues may come through as a bit less easily under-
stood.

Why? Because in life we can't see inside other peoples' heads.

Back when I was a boy, a young man of perhaps eighteen or
twenty lived down the block from us. Though he bothered no one,
he perpetually wandered about at loose ends, jobless and clearly a

bit strange. People felt sorry for his decent, hardworking parents.

Then one day, abruptly, the situation changed. Police appeared with the young man in tow—first questioning his family, then searching a shed behind the house.

Their findings chilled the neighborhood. Unsuspected by anyone, the young man apparently lived a macabre inner life that saw him secretly prowling local cemeteries while his parents assumed him to be asleep. A couple of nights before, he had reopened a grave and mutilated the corpse of a young woman buried that afternoon, removing selected organs in the manner of an inept Jack the Ripper. These he took home and stored in Mason jars in the shed.

It was a situation fit for Robert Bloch or Stephen King, but that's not the point. The issue is that no one suspected that our addled young man, in some private world, was motivated to set to digging in the night-darkened graveyard. His secrets remained secrets until, returning to the cemetery, he was caught in the act of further desecrating the girl's body . . . because none of us could see inside his head.

Another case in point—less gruesome, even if for me almost as disturbing. The incident concerns a man with whom I worked many years ago while editing labor papers. He was president of the union at a local factory. I think I can safely say that we rated as close friends—working together, drinking together, vacationing together, sharing a wide range of interests.

And then, one day, almost by accident, it was discovered that my friend held down a second job, one about which he hadn't shared confidence with me. For he wasn't just a worker or a union president. First and foremost, he was a labor spy, on the payroll of one of the nation's major industrial security agencies. And all those weeks and months I'd thought I'd known him so well, I'd been deceived. Because try as I might, I couldn't get inside his head.

I can't tell you what a cataclysmic shock that was, back in those days when the struggling union movement was fighting to survive. I seldom—maybe not ever—have suffered such a blow. The very fact that it still stands out so sharply in my mind after half a century tells the story.

Nor is my experience unique. Every wife or husband betrayed, every employer who finds that a trusted employee has tapped the till, every parent shattered by the discovery that a son or daughter is doing drugs goes through the same bitter trauma. And "He was always such a good boy," said in regard to assorted serial killers, is a line so familiar it has become almost a litany.

Not that we're talking only of unhappiness or disillusion, you understand. Revelations may be positive as well as negative. Witness the notorious tightwad who, after death, is found to have sponsored dozens of poor students who needed help in financing their educations. The quiet man who's never mentioned military service, but who has the Congressional Medal of Honor tucked in the back of a dresser drawer. The woman with crippling arthritis who conceals her youthful fame as a nationally acclaimed dancer.

(Indeed, my friend Phyllis Whitney, suspense novelist supreme, has projected this to a highly effective plot device. Every major character, she says, should have a secret: some hidden something that he or she doesn't want exposed to the world. She's got a point. But more of that later, in Chapter 6.)

For now, though, the thing to bear in mind is that no matter what you may suspect, you can't really read another person's thoughts or get inside his head.

As a matter of fact, a character either in life or in fiction, may, for his own personal reasons, intentionally convey a false impression.

Item: The girl with the hideously bad disposition who's doing her best to project an aura of sweetness and light until she can land the man she wants.

Item: The man who oozes perfect poise until you discover him weeping in the company restroom.

Item: The woman who wallows in piety for the benefit of her church friends, while on the job she embezzles bank funds.

Item: The friendly retiree whose young manhood included years working in the gas chamber in a Nazi death camp in Poland.

So much subterfuge, so much deceit, so many false impressions.

Yet you, as a writer, can't afford to be taken in by such deceptive masks. Remember, always, that *you* are the creator; first and last, *you* are in control. Deceit and subterfuge are merely tools you use to give your story people depth and interest. Understanding their dynamics, you bring them on as needed, neatly packaged and inserted into characters' heads.

How do you gain the necessary insight into the human reaction process? Specifically, what principles undergird people's — which is to say, characters' — thinking and behavior?

WHAT MAKES PEOPLE TICK?

Shall we start with a basic premise — the one set forth in the summarizing capsule on which we opened? The thing all of us seek, at root, is what we call happiness.

What constitutes happiness? Call it a state of mind that exists in a person when, his bodily needs satisfied, he also feels a sense of self-importance, self-worth.

That sense of self-worth takes all sorts of forms. You find it in an illiterate, immigrant Vietnamese mother who sees her only surviving child graduate from high school. It sparks again when a doctor saves a life . . . a lawyer wins a case . . . a farmer banks the check for a bumper crop . . . a housewife wins a garden show . . . a teenage swinger beds a rock star. It glows in the sense of superiority a carny feels as he short-changes a mark or a vacationing couple boards a plane for Acapulco under the envious eyes of friends who must stay behind. Each finds what, for the moment, he or she calls happiness — "fulfillment of function," in academic gobbledegook. One way or another, each can approve of himself, however briefly. And if others see fit to approve also, so much the better.

Such a state may prove murderously difficult to achieve, however. Why? Because the world and life keep throwing trouble at us — circumstances that block our efforts to attain our goals, shatter our dreams, make us feel helpless and ridiculous and unimportant. Yet in spite of everything, most of us keep striving.

Also, happiness is different things to different people. Inheriting a fortune may, to me, bring only panic at the thought of the responsibilities that will ensue. Or I may so thrill to the excitement of battle that I forget the fear of death.

Too, it may operate on a variety of levels. Witness what's come to be known as the "generation gap." In large measure it sprang from a clash between the traditional concept of "earned happiness" that dominated an earlier period and the "instant happiness" of an affluent society, in which credit cards and bankruptcy filings and singles bars took over. In the past a couple may have attained feelings of self-worth by caring for their elderly parents. Today, some couples seeking instant happiness may consign their parents to a nursing home and get their ego boosts from driving two cars and living in a bigger house. (Which isn't to say, of course, that a nursing home may not be the only answer in many cases.)

Whether these changes in society are good or bad is subject to debate. But the sun has set on the era when women found pride solely in managing a home. Men today are no longer ashamed to be seen changing the baby's diapers or cooking a meal. Some, by choice, stay home as house-spouses, while their wives work outside the home for financial support of the family. And often both spouses must work, just to make ends meet.

Fact is, contemporary marriage no longer follows traditional male/female sexual stereotypes, and your characters had better reflect those changes if you hope to appeal to modern readers.

Unhappiness? That's the other side of the coin, something we all strive to avoid. Call it the loss of self-esteem as a result of disapproval by self or others. Perhaps it springs from a harsh word from the boss, a sidewise glance from a supercilious clerk, the sense of helplessness one feels when a loved one dies, the rage and frustration that comes of a picked pocket, a broken date, a crumpled fender.

But again, each of us is different. The prospect of a visit to the hospital may chill your blood, while I look forward to making such a visit because the anticipated pain will assuage a secret sense of guilt, or give me an excuse to wallow delightedly in self-indulgence, self-pity, or friends' attention. My son-in-law's insults may cut me to the quick, yet bring a certain grim pleasure as I gloat over the shock he's going to get when my will is read.

Now these are things we all experience. Yet in the words of Arthur Conan Doyle's immortal Sherlock Holmes, we see but we do not observe.

This is a luxury which we as writers can't afford. We *must* learn to pay attention to human behavior in all its varied shades and nuances. Most especially, we need to become reflex-familiar with those twists and turns that influence the manner in which people's lives develop. Why? Because they'll provide insight into possible paths our characters may follow and actions they may take.

Is it possible to attack the issue of character dynamics from a different angle? Yes, of course it is. You very well may begin from the assumption that *fear* is the underlying factor. In which case, the question to ask yourself is: What's Character scared of?

Because all of us *are* scared. When the feudist in pioneer Texas cried, "I'll die before I run!" what he really was saying was, "I'm less afraid of death than losing face." And how many times, covering triangle murders, did I hear the line, "We couldn't stand the shame of a divorce" as motive? It's the same peer pressure thing that's sent so many teenagers to death mainlining heroin with their friends.

The person — or the character — may not know he's scared, of course, or if he does, he may not know just what he's scared of. Fear of responsibility may lie at the heart of his secret inner dread, as witness many an educated, once-cultured bum along skid row, many a remittance man in Mexico or Monaco or Marrakesh. I have hypochondriac friends whose blind panic at the thought of disease has immobilized them for life. The fear of failure has locked hundreds, thousands, millions into private cells of never trying. A woman I know was so devastated by Depression poverty that today she lives the life of a virtual indigent though her net worth is more than half a million dollars. And Alfred Hitchcock so feared the possibility of a traffic arrest and jail that he never learned to drive a car.

So much for fear as a dynamic, a source of human conduct. But whether you choose to work from it or from man's never-ending search for fulfillment and happiness, ultimately you'll need to give special consideration to four other concepts: *direction, goal, drive,* and *attitude.*

We'll take them up in the second part of this appraisal of the world within in the next chapter.

6

THE WORLD WITHIN: 2

*How do you keep a character moving?
You point that character towards his
or her private future.*

Each character about whom you write, whether you're aware of it or not, must have a private future. That is, to go back to what we said in Chapter 1, he must care about something, feel that some aspect of his world is important—important enough to fight for.

To that end, and though they can hardly be separated in practice, you need to give him an appropriate *direction, goal, drive,* and *attitude.*

Let's consider each of these separately.

1. DIRECTION: THE ROAD TO HAPPINESS

A character's *direction* may be defined as his tendency to lead the kind of life he enjoys. In effect, it's a sort of unstated search that causes him to seek out experience he finds pleasurable and to act in a manner that fulfills a quite possibly unverbalized "dream of happiness" for him. That this dream may be vague—even nebulous or totally unformulated—is of no consequence. Nor does it matter whether it makes sense to anyone, including the character himself. It still shapes his behavior, just as the alcoholic continues to get drunk despite certain knowledge of the hangover to follow.

Thus, any character, any person—and that includes you, and me, and the woman next door, and the man down the street—lives from infancy to a greater or lesser degree in the grip of an indefinable inner hunger, a gnawing sense that something is missing from his life.

Actually, it may be that what's missing is in the person himself. It's rooted in the sense of inadequacy born of childhood helplessness. What he wants, realize it or not, is to control his life, his destiny.

Not grasping this fact, however, Person — or Character, where fiction is concerned — attempts to fill the void with ego-inflating exploits in the world outside him — his own private combination of what W. I. Thomas, respected sociologist of another day, termed the "four wishes": the human animal's desire for *adventure, security, recognition, response.* (Personally, I'm inclined to add a fifth item, *power,* to the list.) And the way you combine these, the ratio between the elements you zero in on, establishes the direction that you go.

When you translate this into more concrete form, *adventure* comes out as a yearning for new experience, as exemplified in activities ranging from climbing Mount Everest to throwing a brick through a neighbor's window . . . joining the Marines or Peace Corps to signing up for a night course in computer graphics. *Security?* A job with the Postal Service, a bulging bank account, a well-tuned car engine, you name it. Spell *recognition* as fame via election as selectman, winning a breakdance contest, being awarded a scholarship, making headlines with a jailbreak. And *response,* for most of us, equals love on any one of its multitudinous levels: warming to the feeling that someone that counts cares about us. If you want to include *power,* obviously it's exemplified in the authority to hire and fire, the officer's command over his troops, and the woman who includes a potential palimony suit in her armorarium.

So much for the generalities of happiness. More to the point is the way that each of us, consciously or otherwise, selects a certain state or situation as, for us and for the moment, constituting bliss. Call it a symbol, if you will. It's a condition which we subjectively visualize as creating the paradisiacal sense of self-worth/self-importance/self-esteem that we all yearn for.

(Assume that you win such happiness. Is it likely to prove enduring? Not necessarily; indeed, not even likely. The "perfect husband" turns out to be a penny-pincher. The "dream house" floods every time it rains. A failed bank swallows up your nest-egg savings. The town forgets football fame the day you graduate. And that's life, as they say.)

Remember, too, that both in life and in fiction characters operate on separate wavelengths, different levels of intensity. Consider two women, for example. *Slender* equals *happy* where both are concerned. But for whatever reason, *slender* is a compulsion for Woman A. Woman B, on the other hand, finds *slender* in competition with a growling stomach. Result: Woman A stays svelte. Woman B? Fat.

The same principle applies to men, of course. Staying thin is often important in terms of appearance, job promotion, and health. Yet loud are the wails that rise from many as they have to buy new wardrobes because their weight has gone up or down.

Or observe three churchmen—all thoughtful, all dedicated. Religion is important to each—a vital element of their happiness, you might say.

Thus, Bill is not only a believer, but a regular member and attendee.

So is Bob. But in addition to belonging and attending, he sits on the church board.

Bert? A member and attendee too, he has his own private ideas about religion.

Each pays tribute to his faith in a characteristic manner. Bill, for example, follows the rules and is present whenever he's supposed to be.

Bob carries his devotion a step further. Sitting on the board, he plays a definite role in church politics.

Which puts him in direct conflict with Bert, for Bert believes that the church's trend toward modernization and the contemporary is part of the devil's plot to corrupt both the Word of God and the congregation, especially the young.

The result, frequently, is a fine Donnybrook that nearly comes to fisticuffs in the nave. Hot tempers, hot words spill over the sanctuary like blazing oil.

Yet each of these men and women operates from the same basic principle: a yearning for fulfillment, for happiness.

Each symbolizes that happiness differently, however. Thus, Bill enjoys the sense of duty fulfilled that comes with attendance . . . the warm feeling of being active on the right side. As a God-fearing man, he's proud of raising his children in the right path, being head of a Christian family.

Bob, in contrast, isn't content merely to stand up and be counted. A business type and aggressive he wants to help run the show from the church boardroom. It's one of the things that makes him feel that he's important.

Bert's case is a little different. A bit paranoid, he's suspicious of all authority. The church gives him a point of focus. Add to that his conservatism, his feeling that any change is dangerous, and he's an ideal convert for those who feel the trend to modernization is endangering the church itself and springs from Satan.

Three different men, three different personalities and attitudes. And despite what we've said here, any attempt to explain them is guesswork at best, born of our own views as much as of the facts.

Or what about Woman A, with whom we started? What gives her the drive and strength to cut her caloric intake and increase her exercise to the point that she loses weight . . . whereas Woman B, verbalizing the same goals and desires, somehow never gets around to it?

Because no one knows, your guess, your hypothesis — your rationalization, if you will — is as good as that of anyone else.

Assuming, that is, that you don't go at the task and process blindly. You still need to learn all you can about the foundations upon which rationalizations can reasonably be based.

Don't let your reasoning become involved to the point that it destroys credibility, however. Your fictional logic must, after all, reflect the thinking of your audience. Few Americans would accept the sexist orientation of Iran, with its requirements of the veil, the chador, and subservience of women, or our Hispanic maid's idea that the stars caused disease. Likewise, few people today would see as a good father the domineering, razor-strop-wielding male prevalent a hundred years ago.

It's also one thing to build a solid case, another to dive off the deep end in the manner of the British psychoanalyst who argued that Welsh miners' strikes sprang from guilt reactions over their "rape" of Mother Earth.

In general, when setting up your people, you'll find it most productive to explore again the three main areas of human activity: love, work, and society. Place special emphasis on the things we humans strive for: possession of (an object, a person, a status, a state of mind or being), relief from (fear, oppression, humiliation, loss), or revenge for (a slight, a loss, a betrayal), plus all the multitudes of variations and permutations of which you can conceive.

2. GOAL: DISSATISFACTION AS DYNAMIC

A goal exists only in terms of an existing situation.

More specifically, it's born out of *dissatisfaction* with that situation. In other words, it's more specific than direction.

Or, getting back to the capsule with which we opened, there's some aspect of your situation that you'd like to see *changed:* The girl you adore is dating two other men. You'd like to persuade her to limit her attentions to you alone. Which means that your *goal* is to get her to agree to "go steady."

Or, your paycheck just won't cover today's inflationary outgo. So you make it your *goal* to *change* this sad condition by winning a raise.

Or, your divorced sister has moved back home with her three unruly children, driving your aged parents to emotional and financial desperation. Your goal: to get Sister & Co. out again before Mother and Dad collapse or slash their wrists.

Or, you've discovered that one of your superiors in the Defense Department is a mole, a secret Soviet agent. You *must* find which one (*goal*) before he can pass on vital data.

It's also worth pointing out that goals are of two types: *general* and *immediate*.

The issue here rests on the difference between *chronicle* and *story*.

A chronicle is a record of events, a statement of what happened in a given situation: *The king married the princess and they had five children.*

A story is the record of how somebody deals with danger: *The king married the princess and then found she planned to poison him.*

Finding that the new queen plans to poison him constitutes an unacceptable *change* in the king's situation, his state of affairs, and state of mind.

This change gives the king a general goal: to survive the queen's plan.

To reach this *general* goal, the king must attain a whole series of *immediate* goals. First, possibly, he must avoid drinking the flagon of poisoned wine the queen offers him . . . yet do so in such a way as not to reveal he knows what she's up to. To that end, he pretends a courtier's remark has affronted him, flies into a simulation of rage and, with appropriate byplay, flings the flagon at the unfortunate man, then stalks from the hall.

One scene, one immediate goal out of the way. What next?

Afraid to give the queen another chance at him by retiring to their bedchamber, the king goes alone to the castle chapel, allegedly to ask God for forgiveness for his unseemly display of wrath . . . then steal out a secret door to spy on the queen in an effort to find out whether others are conspiring with her in the attempt to kill him: a new immediate goal.

Mysterious masked figures intercept him. Fighting them off, the king barely escapes. But he does glimpse that the queen has a caller, a woman. Which gives him a new immediate goal: Who is the woman? What is her role where the queen is concerned?

Well, you get the idea. Our character's attempt to attain a general goal results in one change after another in his original situation—in effect, each defeat or change creates a *new* situation and so plunges him into pursuit of a series of new immediate goals, each of which involves him in a new scene, a new conflict.

I can't overemphasize the importance of this matter of goals. Why? Because when you strive to attain a goal, you test characters. Only when a story person fights against odds does he demonstrate whether he's worthy of reward—or, to put it on the most practical level, whether he's worthy of readers' attention. It's the key factor behind the old Hollywood question, "Who do we cheer for?" Readers won't cheer, that is offer interest, unless characters—especially key characters—have goals. And if you don't believe me, how many people cheer for a horse grazing in a pasture, as compared with the number who evidence excitement when the same equine's leading the pack at a racetrack?

3. DRIVE: THE "GIVE A HOOT" FACTOR

Drive, as I use the word here, may be defined as inner pressure, the intensity with which a character wants to change or reshape his situation.

It also, again, points up the absolute necessity of building your story around people who have the capacity to care, to feel that something or other's important.

The end product of drive is attainment of a goal. Thus, given a particular goal, is this goal truly important to Character? How highly does he value it? To what extremes is he willing to go in order to attain it?

In brief, does he really give a hoot about it? Because if he doesn't, for all practical purposes he's useless in a story.

This factor of drive is devastatingly important. It's the key ingredient of the vital element we call commitment. Couple it with direction and goal, and you equip yourself with the priceless "desire plus danger" combination that keeps pages turning far into the night. Failure to provide it in major characters can prove the kiss of death where your story is concerned. For regardless of writing skill or literary values, the thing that leads most of us to read is still the age-old question that focuses on the hero as he fights against fate: "Will he succeed or won't he?" Where the overwhelming majority of us are concerned, it remains the most solid foundation upon which to build a story.

This brings up a related question: In life, are most people really motivated? And the answer is, no. Not to bog down in semantics, but the majority of us have *drift*, not drive. That is, we fall into things through happenstance and follow the line of least resistance. The term that best describes our progress is *random*. The job the average person chooses likely is the first one offered. The girl he marries is his sister's friend or his neighbor's daughter or the double date that proves amenable to heavy necking. Given a menu that includes octopus or truffles, he'll choose roast beef and mashed potatoes every time.

Why does one person have drive, another not?

Partly, the issue likely is inertia, or ignorance of a special sort· an inability to grasp the potentialities of impinging situations. Or, call it fear of change, an overweening doubt that change might be beneficial or desirable or fun. Most of us live like Jean Giono's villagers in *Le Moulin de Pologne*: ". . . we fear knives and wild beasts less than a life style which is different from our concept of how life should be," and so automatically answer, "Oh, I couldn't do that!" to most possibilities.

So, most people drift.

Or, as my wife succinctly puts it, "Most of us, most of the time, are impulse buyers in the supermarket of life."

Beyond this, however, can it be that drift, in its own way, constitutes a sort of drive—an unverbalized goal of avoiding the discomfort that comes with involvement and "giving a hoot"?

It seems at least possible to me. Thus, some years ago I knew a handsome, cultured, literate man in his thirties who worked at an extremely routine job in a film library. The tasks assigned him clearly were far below his capacity and everyone knew it.

Finally one Friday afternoon the supervisor called him over.

"Ed," he said, "you rate a better spot than this. I'm promoting you."

"If you do," Ed retorted, not so much as blinking, "then I quit."

"Go on," the super laughed. "You take over as chief of section Monday morning."

"Goodbye," Ed said.

He never came back after the weekend.

What was behind it all? I'll never know, though certainly I've speculated enough. Fear may have been the issue, as when you're afraid you can't deliver what's called for, or when in the past you've made some tragic error and can never forget the possibility of another. Or guilt. Or a private ethical standard that says you shouldn't rise above your fellows. There may even have been a physical angle—ulcers, heart trouble, some nervous disorder.

What about such "drifting" characters where your story is concerned?

That depends. An individual who changes course with every passing breeze may prove perfectly adequate if cast in a bit part—playing a spear-bearer in the chorus, as it were. But at best he'll prove a frail reed; count on it.

Or, as Joseph Campbell has summed up the situation in *The Hero with a Thousand Faces,* "Often in actual life, and not infrequently in the myths and popular tales, we encounter the dull case of the call [to adventure] unanswered; for it is always possible to turn the ear to other interests. Refusal of the summons converts the adventure into its negative. Walled in by boredom, hard work, or 'culture,' the subject loses the power of significant affirmative action and becomes a victim to be saved. . . . All he can do is create new problems for himself and await the gradual approach of his disintegration."

On the other hand, is it possible you can give a character—any character—drive?

Yes. The trick is merely to decide on what Character cares about, what's important to him—and whether he realizes it or not.

Consider a character drifting through life who, without thinking about it, thinks of himself as being honest.

Now, out of a clear blue sky, someone empties the cashbox where he works. Though there's insufficient evidence to convict, circumstances point to Character. In the eyes of those who count ("significant others," in the sociologists' phrase), Character suddenly finds himself reclassified from decent person to probable thief.

Does this bother Character? Of course it does—especially if you build it up properly. All at once it's vital to his emotional well-being that he prove he's innocent; and the only way he can do that is to catch the real thief. Whereupon he not only acquires a general goal but a drive to reach it.

Let's run that by again, a step at a time.

To give a character drive:

1. You devise something for him to care about, consciously or otherwise.
2. You fit him out with a suitable goal, in view of the direction you've postulated for him.
3. You threaten that goal, that something he cares about.
4. You establish reasons for him not to quit, reasons to continue to fight against the threat and reach his goal.

Reasons not to quit may be external, or internal, or both.

You already know about external reasons: The boat is sinking; if Hero doesn't bail or pump he'll drown. Heroine's brother is in the death house; unless she finds evidence to clear him he'll be executed. Things like that.

Internal reasons are the ones inside Character's head. Pride: "I won't crawl." Its reverse, shame: "They mustn't ever know." Duty: "I couldn't let the team down." Gratitude: "He saved my life." Loyalty: "She's my mother." Intense to the point of obsession, they won't allow Character to rest.

How does Character acquire these ideas? And yes, you do need to know. Not to keep you in suspense, they're the product of life-long conditioning, as explained in Chapter 8.

4. ATTITUDE: CHARACTER PLUS HANGUP

What do we mean by *attitude*? To oversimplify, call it a feeling about some situation or subject; a consistent (yet quite possibly irrational) disposition that Character is reluctant to relinquish.

In other words, an attitude is a hangup that's hard to get rid of. A stripper in all likelihood will have one attitude towards men; a Carmelite nun, another. When a pedophiliac organization cries

"Sex before eight or else it's too late," it reveals an attitude towards both sex and children that most of us find revolting.

Similarly, Character may see the world as making steady progress or, contrarily, as going to hell in a handbasket. The younger generation is Earth's hope for the future, or it's the plague that will bring down civilization as we know it. He may stand firm for abortion rights or loathe it as cold-blooded murder of the unborn. He dotes on hot fudge sundaes, or detests them because he believes they give him pimples. Noodling for catfish is great sport, or a species of insanity that may end with a water moccasin chomping on your biceps.

Be sure, however, that a character's attitudes fit his noun. A policeman has one set of attitudes, a lawyer another, a criminal, a third. Same for teacher and student, boss and worker.

Attitudes are products of conditioning, as we'll see in Chapter 8. Meanwhile, just bear in mind that they're not one, but many.

Taken collectively, grouped together, they constitute an entity commonly called *point of view*: a character's generally habitual, to-be-expected reactions to whatever aspects of life and the world that come to his attention in the story. (Note that here I'm using "point of view" in its general meaning of outlook or opinion — not in the technical sense of "viewpoint character," the person from inside whom the reader experiences the story as it happens. That approach is correct when you're setting up your material for presentation to your reader. But the writer himself needs to be aware of the thinking and feeling of *all* his story people, each and every one, not just that of the key figure.)

Each major character's attitude is something that you as a writer need to understand, though not on a definitive level, necessarily. That kind of study would call for long-time scrutiny. The broad outlines will be enough, with occasional sidetrips into the swamps and bayous of personality to add color and interest.

In particular, you'll need to become aware of the special areas of mind and thought that your story brings into focus.

You can do worse than to term this collective pattern your character's *dominant attitude*.

Thus, in a romance, Female Lead's dominant attitude very well may center on the way she sees — and, in action, reacts to and behaves towards — men. Are they dominating bullies, like her boss? Frail reeds, in the manner of her hopeless, helpless uncle? Eternal womanizers who zero in on every passing skirt? Shadow images of her boastful, bragging brother? Potential sources of security via marriage? Tender father figures in whom she can find solace? Romantic heroes to thrill and excite her? Stalwart partners for a lifetime of warmth and peace? The list could go on and on.

In a science fiction story, in contrast, Hero's dominant attitude very well might revolve around his conviction that the human race is doomed—or will only be saved—by continued psychic interbreeding with superior aliens from beyond the galaxy.

The suspense novel character? Perhaps, cynically, he looks out on a world of potential victims. Whoever he meets, male or female, he always sees johns or suckers. Or, conversely, he naively finds good in the most hardened villains and stands convinced that he must capture them in order to help them see the light. And the character in the tale of the occult may be totally conditioned by his belief in clairvoyance or reincarnation or the Great God Ptath or the writings of H. P. Blavatsky.

Nor is application of this principle limited to genre fiction. Mainstream books abound in which characters live in the past, or are forever racked by jealousy or greed or family pride or worry or the compulsion to do the right thing no matter what the consequences. Sholem Asch offers excellent examples in his best-selling *East River.* Moshe Wolf Davidowsky is an orthodox Jew striving to practice his faith in the new world and pass on Old World traditions to his children. His every action and thought are dominated by his attempt to follow his religious beliefs. Patrick McCarthy, in turn, reflects his Irish Catholic upbringing in his violent hatred of Jews. Can such conflicting values survive when Moshe Wolf's son, Irving, marries Patrick's daughter, Mary? It's Old World attitudes in the parents, confronted with New World attitudes in the children.

Further, a dominant attitude quite possibly may be modified by other coexisting—and quite possibly conflicting—attitudes, for few of us are all of a piece. The example that comes to mind concerns a friend of mine, a United Auto Workers official. He was outspoken in his belief in racial equality. Only a trip with him to the Pacific Northwest, where he grew up, revealed that while equality for Blacks was fine, Filipinos were another matter!

In other words, circumstances alter cases, so be sure you've considered all pertinent angles before you slap on labels. Thus, a character may have one dominant attitude in one story—that is, one particular set of circumstances. But another, different situation may bring a different attitude into focus.

Note too that this business of character dynamics, what goes on inside a given story person's head, is not necessarily revealed to readers save in terms of the way the character behaves. You, in contrast, *must* know Character's thought patterns and propelling forces in that story, if the story is to make sense. Hemingway offers some brilliant examples. Or reread Dashiell Hammett's *The Maltese Falcon*. At no point are you given any hint of what Sam Spade is thinking, save in terms of speech and action. But clearly, Hammett as the author had to know.

HOW MUCH DO MOTIVES MATTER?

Meet Pam. She's a lovely girl.

Her boyfriend, Terry, is the be-all and end-all of her existence. And as she'll tell you, with or without provocation, her life's ambition is to marry him.

So far, so good. Pam has a goal-motivated drive, a purpose. That's a big step forward in equipping her to become a major character in a story.

Next question: What about her private world, the world inside her head?

Or, to capture it in a word, what's her *motivation?*

It's at this point that I take a somewhat different track than do most analysts of fiction. Because I tend to draw a line between motive and purpose.

Purpose, as I see it, is what a character wants to *do:* kiss a girl, take a trip, go to church, rob a bank, rescue a baby from a burning building. In brief, purpose is something you can *take action* to accomplish.

Motive, on the other hand, is *why* Character wants to do something. And often, not even the person himself understands the reason or reasons behind it, as witness the old line about "the devil made me do it." Or, to put it another way, more often than not, motive is *rationalization.*

Thus, Pam. Her purpose: to marry Terry.

Her motive? Ah, now, that's a different matter! *Maybe* she wants to marry him because she loves him. Or maybe it's because he makes good money, or because he's a neat dancer, or because she wants a child, or because she's pregnant, or because she's now thirty-one and her mother keeps nagging her about spinsterhood, or because she fears people will find out she's a closet lesbian, or because she's developed a warped notion that the insignificant bump on her nose (hereditary with her dead father's people, her mother tells her) makes her unattractive to acceptable men. (Actually, they're not even aware of it.) Thing is, no one, not even Pam, will ever really know her motives. Not for sure.

The point to all this is that *purpose* is external-oriented, action-oriented, "to do"-oriented. It's born of direction and drive and attitude.

Motive, in contrast, is an internal, private world, rationalization kind of thing.

For you as a writer, the key issue is to be sure that any major character has a goal, a purpose, no matter how far out in left field it may be, so long as it seems logical to Character at the time. After which, you reach inside Character's head and select an appropriate excuse for her having it (motive, right?) and endow her with properly compelling pressures that force her to keep striving to attain it, physical and emotional reasons why she can't quit.

May this process start from either end? Yes, of course. You're playing God for the duration of your tale, so if you prefer to begin with motive, the "Why?" approach, it's perfectly acceptable that you do so. From a practical standpoint, however, ordinarily your task will prove infinitely easier if you begin with goal, with purpose, than if you wander off through a morass of pre-assigned motives. The trick is to decide what you want or need your character to do in order to move your story in the direction you want it to go. Then rationalize the necessary "whys."

And while it may appear I speak only of "major" characters above, this principle applies to *all* your story people, not just heroes, heroines, and villains. The issue is merely the degree to which you develop the picture.

Have we said enough about the world inside your characters' heads? More than enough, quite possibly, since the thing that really counts is your own work, your personal gropings and experiments and (sorry) failures.

Be that as it may. Just bear in mind that in shaping up any given character, and regardless of whether or not you reveal it to your readers, it's vital that you provide him with a private inner world compounded of direction, goal, drive, and attitudes. Without such you'll have trouble to spare when you try to predict his conduct in your story.

In addition, you'll need to know how to bring your man or woman to life with words on the printed page. You'll learn a proven approach to doing it when you turn the page to Chapter 7, "The Breath of Life."

7

THE BREATH OF LIFE

*How do you bring a character to life?
You make the character reveal emotion.*

Our most revealing moments are those in which we experience stress.

What's stress? Mental tension springing from emotion.

What's emotion? To oversimplify, it's liking or disliking, feeling good or feeling bad about something.

Emotion, feeling good or feeling bad about something, is what gives a character direction. If something gives him pleasure, he seeks it out. If it gives him pain, he avoids it.

Direction is what makes us aware that a character is alive. Without it, a person or a character is a vegetable—eating and breathing and existing, perhaps, but going nowhere.

Herewith, a mousy little man, Mr. Holcomb. A wimp, a nonentity, a nothing. So far as most of us are concerned, he might as well not exist.

Only then, one day, something leads Mr. Holcomb into a display of emotion. Something makes him mad or glad—the neighborhood hoodlum drives a car across Mr. Holcomb's freshly seeded lawn, let's say. Or the woman across the street towards whom Mr. Holcomb has entertained tentatively amorous thoughts presents him with a spectacular Valentine's Day cake. Or the sister who's his only living relative dies. Something like that. At which point Mr. Holcomb screams or beams or hangs himself. And because this is so, all at once he exists . . . takes on a new dimension and acquires a focus.

Why? You already know the answer: Mr. Holcomb cares about something, so he reacts to something that affects it.

In a word, emotion has brought him to life.

Or consider Alice Withers, the woman in the shabby house on the corner. Old and pale and without color, she is, in a word, another nonentity. But unknown to those about her, somewhere deep inside she still feels.

Then something stress-provoking happens: The husband who deserted her thirty years ago comes back.

Joyously, Alice welcomes him to her bed.

And cuts his throat.

Instantly, as in the case of Mr. Holcomb, Alice comes to life for us. We're fascinated by her. She's enveloped in a pulsing cloud of speculation, gossip.

And all because, all at once, she's displayed emotion.

Actually, the issue isn't just that the person involved has revealed emotion. It's *because,* in showing emotion, she's roused emotion in us too. By feeling strongly, she's led us to feel also.

Indeed, this is what *empathy* means. It says that we *feel with* another.

In helping readers to empathize with story people, you as a writer are selling them emotion . . . your ability to rouse feelings in them, good or bad.

Feelings come in all shapes and sizes. Quite possibly the reader who's totally disenchanted with blood and violence or purple passion will respond with great waves of throbbing nostalgia to your description of a sagging, gray-weathered Ozark farmhouse at dusk. And though often overlooked, fragments of daily routine or ineptitude or stupidity that we ourselves have experienced can go a long way towards helping us to feel warmth and sympathy for a character.

The message here is that it's to your advantage to consider the tastes and prejudices of your particular audience. Are you writing for men or for women? For "young adults" or the *Modern Maturity* set? For people who love pets and rural life or apartment dwellers? It does make a difference!

Also, most readers prefer fiction that rouses their emotions and evokes their feelings as soon as possible. They seek the promise that something interesting—that is, emotion-provoking—is going to happen, and the sooner the better.

To this end, most writers tend to try to capture their readers' attention ("hook" them, in the parlance) quickly.

A hook may be defined as a scene at the beginning of a story that is striking and self-explanatory and plunges some character (the hero or heroine, preferably) into danger in a manner that intrigues your readers.

Ordinarily, you do this by raising the fear that something will or won't happen. For example, in the film *Jaws,* a picture that concerns the menace of a shark in a beach area, the shark is introduced early. The hint of disaster to come is riveting beyond escape. Other ploys that have proved highly successful at one time or another include the case of the hero who awakens to find a murdered girl sharing his bed or a deadly coral snake coiled on his bare stomach. And the play that opens with a sinister character surreptitiously planting a bomb under the sofa on which other characters take seats moments later allegedly is surefire theater.

Or if you prefer something less redolent of blood-and-thunder, there's always the "springboard scene" to fall back on. In its simplest form it, in effect, relies on a character engaged in some motivated action, whether or not it's apparently related to the overall story. What counts is that it presents Character as having direction, being involved in some exhibition of relatively inconsequential purpose, which builds into a scene that puts the character in a position to be endangered; his ordered existence is disrupted. You see it when Heroine telephones her boyfriend, but gets a wrong number — another, different man. Or when Hero, opening his mail, spills $500 from an envelope that bears no return address. Or when, hearing an ambulance siren, someone goes to the window — just as said ambulance brakes to a halt in front of the house. What counts is that you present a character who has direction, some pattern of existence, which is interrupted by a change that forces him or her to make an adjustment.

(Would you rather make your readers smile? A TV commercial not long ago showed a boy racing to his girl's house under the delusion that her parents were away. But when he rings the bell, her father opens the door. Which demonstrates that danger can be a happening that merely disrupts anticipation.)

Why is this such a useful pattern? First and foremost, because every story is the record of how somebody deals with danger.

One way or another, *every change constitutes a danger.* And yes, I do include the situations of every father who finds his young daughter has tied up the bathroom, every mother who discovers that someone's turned off the oven while the cake is baking, every boy who finds his date has stood him up, every girl who learns the job she sought has gone to the boss's daughter.

The point is that change demands that we adjust, adapt to a new set of rules, a different circumstance. But we may not be able to make that adjustment successfully, no matter how minor the alteration demanded appears. Therefore, it constitutes a threat and potentially holds danger. The more important the *status quo* is to a character, the greater the emotion it will evoke.

This is not to say that an initial change may seem to be of particular consequence. Quite possibly it will appear to be, at best, trivial . . . then lead into another event or events that reflect pure trauma. Witness a New York friend of mine, who coming out of an office building in heavy rain, was deluged by gutter water when a cab swerved to the curb. His pants were so soaked he couldn't make what turned out to be a vital meeting.

(A side note: It's axiomatic in fiction writing that it's permissible to use coincidence to get your hero *into* trouble, never to get him *out*.)

Am I exaggerating the chances of such things happening? Of course. But it's the way you must learn to think if you're to be a writer. Indeed, it seems to me, one of the most vital qualities for a writer to have is an ability to see the potentialities of impending doom in everything that happens.

This is not to say that your writing must present emotion in supercharged terms. To the contrary. In humor, or stories told with a light touch (the old Craig Rice mysteries come to mind) the wry and the whimsical frequently work better than does the heavy-handed. But the emotion, the like/dislike factor, is still there, no matter how masked with drollery.

Emotion also may lie screened in apparently non-emotional material. Many of Dell Shannon's books offer fine cases in point. The writing at first appears flat, uncolored, stripped of feeling— strictly work-a-day reporting. Yet the facts, the details cited, in themselves accumulate to draw a response from readers. Why? Because we, the audience, are pre-conditioned to react to certain things in a certain way—that is, with certain emotions. The very fact of death or sex or potential danger or humiliation evokes feeling. A character's behavior in a situation involving a dog or a baby or an aged couple both characterizes the character and creates emotion. So does portrayal of frustrations, as when someone has trouble repairing a faucet, raising tropical fish, or coping with a rebellious seven-year-old ... because readers have themselves been frustrated. (As a bonus, it also provides human touches and so builds identification and empathy.)

What counts most of all, however, is that your major characters somehow exhibit purpose and show direction.

Indeed, to reiterate, Character doesn't necessarily need to know he has a goal. Quite possibly it will be enough if he simply behaves *as if* he's trying to attain an objective: the boy who "accidentally" breaks a dish he doesn't want to wipe, or clowns in an unconscious effort to attract a girl's attention; the man who consistently fails when thrust into a job he feels too much for him; the woman who, convinced that she's unattractive, dresses in a manner that stresses her bad points. We all can think of a dozen cases from life without even trying. The issue is, when action clashes with words, we judge a man by what he does, not what he says — and the same principle applies in fiction.

However, a central character, a hero, ordinarily will prove more satisfactory and easier to work with if he's consciously trying to do something, accomplish something — that means he's trying to change some aspect of the situation with which he's confronted and meets with trouble in the process.

One reason for this is that more emotion — that is, interest — is generated when goal-oriented effort is frustrated than when routine action simply goes in a straight line, with no complicating problems.

To try to accomplish anything, change anything, Character must of necessity be in the grip of some emotion. He must *feel* — he must feel like doing something, or *not* doing it.

Anything that *doesn't* make him so feel, that doesn't arouse a drive to do or not do whatever it is, isn't worth putting in your story.

How do you create emotion in a character?

The best way is to start by feeling the emotion yourself. To that end, search your own background for moments in which you felt strongly.

Such moments don't necessarily have to be related to your character or your story. It's enough that *you* felt.

Can you recall a moment when you were so angry at someone that you wished you could kill him? *Really* wished it, on a level that made your fists tremble and your jaws ache and tears come to your eyes?

Live through that moment again now, in emotional memory. Paint a picture of it in your mind's eye. Experience the tension, the dryness of your mouth, the smell of dust or perfume or sweat or tobacco or burning bacon. Were your hands wet or dry, your vision clear or rage-blurred, your brain racing or frozen or racked with pain sharper than any migraine? What was said or done that triggered your reaction—not in broad-brush generalities, but in detail?

Then, assign some of those same feelings to your character, selecting and arranging them for impact, capturing them in words so your readers will experience them as you did.

Do the same for other frozen fragments of time you've lived through: the anguished hour of your father's death; the excitement you felt as the bobsled hurtled down Joker's Hill or you shot the pier at Gray's Beach on your surfboard; the panic when you knew for sure your car was going to crash; the way your heart pounded when the new boy kissed you; the shame when the principal caught you smoking in the restroom. The list goes on and on. . . .

Where you the writer are concerned, just hunting for such bits that will make you—and your character—feel is a worthwhile enterprise.

Recognize, too, that when you "take an interest" in something, that means you have a feeling about it. You're experiencing emotion.

Boredom? It's what you feel when you wish you were doing something else. Even if you don't know what that something is.

Any goal is, of necessity, rooted in emotion. If you don't know what that emotion is, ask yourself the simple question raised in earlier chapters: *Why doesn't he quit?*

The answer will breathe life into your characters, I promise.

This is perhaps a good place to take up the matter of how to control reader reaction to each of your story people. It's important and I've discussed it at some length in my earlier books, *Techniques of the Selling Writer* and *Film Scriptwriting: A Practical Manual.* But here, especially, in regard to the problem of characterization, we need to give reader reaction close attention.

So, how do you create characters readers will like?

To begin with, the character who turns us on is somehow like us. Not necessarily physically like us, you understand, but like in terms of attitudes and standards and beliefs, the things we care about and feel to be important.

Thus, if you accept and approve of monogamy, higher education, water fluoridation, or vegetarianism, you'll feel more at home with others who agree with you and share those beliefs, rather than with outspokenly promiscuous swingers, hillbillies who think any schooling beyond readin'-'ritin'-'rithmetic is a waste of time, dedicated anti-Communists who consider fluoridation a Soviet plot, or enthusiastic carnivores. So while you may tolerate life in a society that places you side by side with those who hold such opposing views, you're not likely to enjoy reading stories that feature heroes or heroines who mirror such lifestyles and whose behavior is diametrically opposite to your standards.

Many readers today can't identify with a virtue-for-virtue's-sake attitude in a heroine, or rejection of a little marijuana at a party, or the concept of sacrificing years of a life to repay a debt. All these have been used successfully in the past, but will they prove successful today, in view of changing audience mores? It's a vital question, and one you certainly need to bear in mind as you plan your stories.

This is *not* to say that a hero or heroine must share *all* your beliefs and attitudes. Quite possibly Hero is a bank robber or con man; Heroine, a *femme fatale* on a mission of assassination. But each holds, in addition, some aspect of outlook in common with Reader; some feeling with which Reader can identify, as when Hero is deeply concerned about his mother's welfare or Heroine yearns for home and children. It's the old familiar prostitute-with-a-heart-of-gold pattern, the murderer who worships his wife or loves his dog.

But fiction that merely portrays people as being like you isn't enough for a character—especially a successful leading character. Such a story person must not only be like us, he must be like us *and more,* in the same way Superman is like us, and more.

Specifically, Character must be larger than life in that he takes on challenges over and beyond us. To that end, he must have a quality that, secretly, we all wish we had but frequently do not.

That component is *courage,* the kind of courage that enables Hero to challenge the fate life has dealt him in the story.

Not that this quality will necessarily be labeled as courage, you understand. But it's there implicitly, in the fact that Character reacts as he does when faced with what appears to be certain disaster. It's captured in the old verse born of scripture:

> *Dare to be a Daniel,*
> *dare to stand alone.*
> *Dare to have a purpose firm;*
> *dare to make it known.*

Such courage raises Character above the crowd (even if you don't necessarily say so to your readers) and gives him the strength to fight on, win or lose. Where most of us would back down, give up, surrender, he refuses to accept defeat. Faced with the safe that can't be cracked, he cracks it. Forbidden to seek answers to dark questions, he turns the spotlight on them. Cataclysm is a thing he meets head-on, as well as all the lesser levels of trouble that spring from the pattern of change on which your story is built.

Such courage is something we all yearn for. It binds us to a story with chains of envy for the larger-than-life character who has it. Consciously or otherwise, we thrill at the idea of being like him, so the story in which he appears provides us with that pleasurable release of tension the psychologists call catharsis.

This pattern is at the heart of the phenomenon of reader identification—an often misunderstood term that means only that the behavior of a character in the story situation is such that it excites and fascinates readers and leaves them feeling satisfied with the story's resolution.

Further, a frequently overlooked aspect of this picture is that readers don't identify with just *one* character in a story. At various points and for various periods, the behavior of other story people may take the spotlight as they exhibit intriguing behavior and cold nerve, so that Reader identifies with each of them in turn also.

To conceive a character redoubtable enough to take on such challenges may require you to scrutinize Character's past history, his background. For techniques for so doing, check out the next chapter, "Bent Twigs."

8

BENT TWIGS

*How much background should
you give a character?
Only enough to make your reader —
and you — believe in him.*

Herewith, a character. He has a proper label, plus an inner world. And he's fleshed out with appropriate tags, traits, relationships, and preoccupations.

Next question: What has shaped him so?

The answer, of course, is his background. To understand the present and future, explore the past.

So, you give Character a background.

Where does said background come from?

From you, of course. You, the writer, the creator.

Why? Because to write effectively about a character, you yourself must understand people enough that you can devise a believable background for your character.

Understanding people is what this chapter's all about.

Understanding can spring only from an awareness of key elements in Character's background — that is to say, Character's roots, regardless of whether or not you choose to reveal these roots to your readers.

Or, to put it another way, your rationalization of each character and his or her behavior will make sense only if Character has a past.

How much past?

No more than is necessary to make Character's emotional state clear to your readers.

This is how it works:

In most instances a person's set, his attitudes, are learned behavior, based on long-time conditioning . . . repetition of an experience or pattern over and over. But for story purposes a certain degree of simplification and dramatization is not only warranted, but well-nigh essential. To this end, you as a writer need to try to tie Character's key attitude in any incident to a single, memorable, past event, insofar as possible.

If you can capture that formative event in a mental picture, a sensory snapshot that tends to flash into Character's mind's eye any time he thinks about Event, so much the better.

Your story requires, for example, that a man be thrown into a state of hysterical panic. You need a credible reason for said panic. So, you hunt through possible rationalizations that might fit the circumstance, the story.

Well, plenty of people are well-nigh paralyzed at even the thought of contact with snakes. So how about introducing a snake? One way or another, you can find a plausible excuse—rationalization, that is—for the reptile that will make sense within the plot line's framework.

Next question: *Why* does this particular person react so strongly to serpents?

Answer: You—the writer, the rationalizer—decide that, back in Character's childhood, a sadistic older sister, resenting him and vindictive, acquired a three-foot garter snake on a biology field trip. Waiting till Little Brother's asleep that night, she drapes the snake across his face, then pricks his neck with a teasing needle.

Brother wakens. The snake writhes across his face. Screaming, clawing, convulsing, Brother goes into psychic trauma on a level so deep that it still lives with him today.

You the writer put this into words—a sensory image that recaptures the moment as Brother experiences it in the present:

> *The snake—!*
>
> *In a flash he was back in the blackness of that other night so long ago—feeling the needle-sting below his jaw; the dry, scaly coils writhing across his face; the terror erupting into a sound . . .*
>
> *Warren's control exploded. Lurching backward, arms flailing, he screamed: a raw, unintelligible, incoherent cry.*

Do you get the idea, overwritten and corny as the presentation may be? Background, past history, prior experience, now undergirds rationalization, so readers believe it and read on.

Obviously, and despite this example, extremes are by no means essential. The fragrance of a particular shaving lotion may turn a girl's thoughts from the man she's with to her father. Whereupon, her reactions will be those you wish to evoke: favorable, if the sensory image called forth is of her kind, good father tenderly stroking her hair as she cries over a bruised knee; unfavorable, if the picture that flashes through her mind is of a womanizing father preparing for an extramarital liaison while her mother sobs in the blinding pain of an appendicitis attack.

Clearly, you don't have to spell out the reasons for everything your story people do, you understand. For bit players, and sometimes even those more important, it's often enough that a character simply have a fear of heights or a love of fudge or a belief in ghosts, *sans* explanations. But if you do need backup for your rationalizations — well, now you have a tool to help you handle the problem.

What if you want to keep Mysterious Mike's thought processes a secret, at least for the time being, or if you're not in his viewpoint? One approach is to state it cold turkey, as an author describing a bit of business: "Grimly, Talley scrubbed his hands. Endlessly, it seemed. 'Germs,' he said between clenched teeth. 'They're dangerous. I know. I watched my cousin die of anthrax.'"

Another device is to let other story people speculate: "I wonder why she did that. I don't care much for garlic either. But to slap a guy's face just because it's on his breath . . ."

Or present the pertinent data subjectively, in Character's viewpoint, as we did with Warren and the snake.

Where do you find the sensory images you need to bring off this kind of thing?

There are the obvious sources, of course. The newspapers and magazines and books you read, the plays and movies and television shows you see. The people you meet, the trips you take, the jobs you've worked at.

Beyond this, however, and above all, probe your own past, then meld the bits and pieces you recall from early childhood. They'll have a color and ring of truth nothing else can match.

Then, when you use these fragments, make them important to your characters by assigning each memory a lesson learned or an emotion evoked, in keeping with the rationalization to which you link it for story purposes.

Remember, too, that reader recall is short, so don't hesitate to make an emotional habit pattern a running gag. Wave it as a tag, as described in Chapter 4. Quite possibly you'll want to have Character feel pain or tenderness or rage every time he encounters a foo dog or Dali painting or blue-eyed blonde. Maybe he doesn't even know why. But *you* know—because you've rationalized it, thought up reasons why it's so, things and events from the past that account for it.

And that's the basic principle of handling background.

"Background" is a term that covers a lot of ground, however. To make it less intimidating, more comprehensible, let's break it down into four elements: body, environment, experience, and ideas.

Do bear in mind, though, that while we may segment "background" for analytical purposes, it remains a whole where character—and life—are concerned. The human animal is a unit, an entity, not bits and pieces. Such organic unity emphasizes consistency, and consistency is the essential element in any character, any personality, no matter how disparate or unlikely of association its components may seem at first glance.

With this disclaimer, let us move on to consider the segments from which a character's background is assembled . . . the jigsaw that forms the basis for his being the way he is.

HOW TO BUILD A BACKGROUND

You build a character's background for three main reasons:

1. You want to make the character unique.
2. You want to give the character reasons for behaving as he does.
3. You want to make him believable, to give him depth.

Failure to develop background, in turn, frequently will result in caricature, the kind of characterization you get in cartoons, in which the obvious is so exaggerated as to result in easily recognized but ludicrous distortion. It can be useful for minor characters, bit players. But the picture that emerges will hardly resemble real people.

At the same time, don't overload characters with background. As was pointed out earlier, a character is a *simulation* of a human being, not the real thing. Bear down too heavily on his or her past history, and it takes over. The story stops, and your reader becomes confused or bored. And that, you can't afford!

In any case, and regardless of whether or not you introduce the information you develop into the actual story, there's no better technique for evoking it in yourself than to probe Character's background, assigning the elements that have shaped him into the individual he is today. Knowing that he marched with Mad Mike Hoare in Katanga, or that his grandmother introduced him to *War and Peace* when he was four, or that he pledged himself to the church at age seven can't help but give him dimension as you think his story through.

Your first step, of course, is to decide on the role Character plays — the things he has to do, the functions he has to perform.

Check this against each of the four components of background: body, environment, experience, and ideas.

Finally, choose and build up pertinent aspects from each, in terms of incidents, anecdotal bits, word pictures that create the impression you want Character to make on your readers.

You seek to convince Reader that Character is cruel and vicious, for example. So, you introduce an incident in which Character recalls the pleasure he felt when he revenged himself on his sister for some imagined slight by lying about her to her boyfriend, or destroying undelivered the letter that offers her a better job, or poisoning her beloved dog.

Or maybe you don't introduce it. But just by the process of conceptualizing it you create a picture in your own mind and a reaction to Character that will help you on a subconscious level to select, arrange, and describe the current action in a manner that will evoke the response you seek from readers.

BODY: THE PLACE IT ALL STARTS

Body begins with history — or, to put it in more specific terms, ancestry — heredity, genetic roots.

Does ancestry make a difference? It does indeed. We all know that some of us are brighter than others, with a spread that extends from the "transcendent mental superiority" of a da Vinci or Einstein or Francis Bacon to the slavering helplessness of the hopelessly retarded. Heredity is what makes a dwarf a dwarf, while a Watusi grows to seven feet tall. Diabetes, allergic asthma, epilepsy, sickle cell anemia—all tend to take their toll from one generation to another. Ancestry is why most Blacks have kinky hair and Balts have blue eyes. Genetic twists pop forth in Down's syndrome and hemophilia and phenylketonuria and thin enamel on teeth. And where would Dracula have been had he not had his vampire forebears?

Indeed, the old nature-versus-nurture controversy is far from dead, for recent studies indicate that such traits as timidity, risk-seeking, aggressiveness, vulnerability to stress, and obedience to authority may be inherited, at least in part, rather than being the product of conditioning.

Beyond this, there's the body of the character himself: the specific physical equipment with which he's endowed. Thus, the pretty girl sees the world through different eyes than does her plainer sister, because her conditioning has accustomed her to being flattered and deferred to—perhaps spoiled. Consequently, she responds in a different manner. Depending on other modifying factors, she may consider a request for a date from a boy who can afford only hamburgers an insult. Or, she may look upon it as an opportunity to prove her egalitarianism and social consciousness. But she's unlikely simply to be grateful that someone's asked her, the way her homely sibling might.

In the same way, the six-foot athlete is used to one kind of treatment, the five-foot bookworm another. The man hailed as "Fats" doesn't have the same outlook as the one called "Slats." And can anyone doubt that the size of Cyrano de Bergerac's nose played a role in shaping his personality? Would Long John Silver have been the same man had he not lost a leg? Was Quasimodo influenced by his hump, Superman by his indestructibility? And Theresa (in *Looking for Mr. Goodbar*), deformed by childhood polio—how would you rate the handicap as a factor in her murder?

Deafness creates a behavior pattern unlike that of the blind or nearsighted or cross-eyed. The stutterer's speech may turn him into a recluse or a Demosthenes. Would Captain Hook have been as cold-hearted had he not lost his hand? Dyslexia and the learning problems that go with it may turn a happy child into a delinquent.

Or consider the plight of a high school friend of mine. His father had a clubfoot. The father, growing up in the Wabash River bottoms, had spent endless winter hours sitting at ice-edge—frustrated, freezing—watching friends skate. For him, the sport became a symbol for all the fun his handicap denied him.

As an adult, he still saw skating through a roseate haze, as irrational as it was glowing. When his wife bore him a son, he couldn't wait for the child to grow old enough to glide over the ice at the local rink.

The problem was that the son, far from fulfilling his father's dreams, detested skating. He hated the cold, the falls, the loss of hours when he wanted to be doing other things.

The father couldn't understand such an attitude. He harangued his son endlessly about it. Result: bitterness, on a level that left a permanent breach between them.

All of which is merely another way of saying that circumstances alter cases, and different groups and societies hold to different standards. Witness the bound feet of Chinese women in the days of the empire and the scarification and tattooing of Melanesian Islanders. Each is prized in its own setting—and makes no sense elsewhere.

When creating story people give attention, too, to such factors as *age, sex,* and *health.*

Thus, a child's response is different than that of an adult. The teenage girl who, on a dare, dances nude in a car's headlights on a country road, seldom would repeat the performance at forty. At twenty a sailor may glory in his tattoos; at fifty, he pays through the nose to have them removed. The oldster who once reveled belligerently in his strength now may tend to walk wide around conflict or heavy manual labor, simply because he recognizes the limitations the years have put on him.

Attitudes, too, change with age. Wasn't it George Bernard Shaw who said that anyone under thirty who wasn't a revolutionary was a dolt, whereas anyone over that age who still so believed rated as a fool?

Similarly, where sex is concerned, girls used to be conditioned to react differently to the world and to life than were boys. In present society, however, although we all know women and men are different, they no longer are quite as different as they once were. Women today can drive eighteen-wheeler semis. They can work in mines or manage international corporations and do a host of things which were unthinkable a generation ago. Even though you still can find female subservience and male machismo, a housewife now is usually such by choice. She almost certainly is aware that other options are available to her.

Health? The man racked with arthritis or asthma or ulcers lives in a different world than the one who claims he's "never had a sick day in my life." Malaria or diabetes or dysentery shape their victims' thinking. So do the colds that continually drag some of us down. Vigor views exertion one way; debility, another.

Yes, body indeed does make a difference!

ENVIRONMENT: VERY SPECIAL WORLDS

Milieu is a word I like. Because while, technically, it's defined as *environment* or *surroundings*, it implies a great deal more.

Specifically, it captures the feeling not just of setting or landscape, but of a society; a social as well as a physical locale. Growing up in San Francisco implies more than just the Golden Gate, Pacific Park, and Union Square. Life in the Mississippi Delta is one thing; that in a Pennsylvania Amish community, another. And double that in spades for a past in the slums of Juarez, the singles bars of New York's Upper West Side, or a French convent.

Such social settings reach out to embrace people as well as geography. They mold the various strata of society that fix standards, for mutually accepted norms and rules are the glue that bonds any group or class together. Shared customs, which clothes are acceptable for which occasions, and how to behave in church or mosque or synagogue are what create a society.

Even more so are accepted modes of thinking. Is it permissible in your private world to say that you hate your brothers and sisters, or to consider rape or murder as a solution to your problems? Are you allowed to show curiosity about your neighbors' affairs or about taboo topics? May you look a person you respect in the eye, or does politeness demand that your gaze be downcast?

Mere physical boundaries of a society have little to do with determining what behavior is considered acceptable. Witness the Thugs of India, those devout stranglers who killed in the name of the Goddess Kali. Joining bands of travelers, they murdered as prescribed by their religion—because they existed as a society within a society, a separate strand within the overall fabric of Indian life.

Or, if India strikes you as too far afield to wander, how about the confidence men and pocket-picking "whiz mobs" in our own land? And certainly it should come as no shock to anyone to discover that a girl whose mother is a whore and who grows up in a brothel may prove promiscuous, or that a boy from a street gang finds nothing immoral about theft. (If you want a good picture of this, read Nicholas Pileggi's *Wiseguy*. It may change the way you think about rehabilitation.) Send a child to school where more than fifty percent of the students smoke pot, and odds are that he or she soon will come to see drug use as acceptable relaxation and recreation.

The same principle applies where more acceptable behavior is concerned. Members of the American Bar Association hold to one orientation, those of the American Medical Association another. Yet both also "belong" to the larger society that is the United States.

Creating a character, you need to ask yourself, "To what societies does this person give allegiance? What do these groups demand of him? Do they involve implicit beliefs and standards that might affect my story, yet be overlooked?"

Special problems arise if your story line calls for Character to change from one stratum, one milieu, to another. Thrusting a thief into "straight" society gives birth to situations that can be comic, or tragic, or both. The maid or farm girl trying to flounder through a world of Main Line "old money" brings automatic confusion and conflict. So does the conscientious objector somehow trapped into military service. A Costa Rican street boy, brought to the U.S. as an adoptee at age thirteen, may be overwhelmed by the wealth he sees here, to the point that he can't resist helping himself to tempting objects regardless of who they belong to. Social workers and counselors drawn from American middle class society, on the other hand, may have trouble understanding that he has no notion of "right" or "wrong" within the framework of his new home's standards. And how many times have writers of novels and screenplays alike teamed professors or such with strippers, to the delight of the public?

Which is why you should never forget that each of your story people is a product of his or her milieu . . . a social as well as a physical environment. The child of a rich, powerful family will think and act differently than will the youngster of the poor and helpless.

This being the case, you yourself must of necessity (1) know the rules and conduct patterns that govern behavior in that particular setting; (2) know the degree to which Character follows these rules;

and (3) know whether your story takes place in that milieu or a divergent one.

Then, develop people to fit, assigning them to their roles with appropriate consideration of their backgrounds. And if you take that to mean that it might not be wise to write about a mafia don or a sugar beet farmer or a fashion model unless you know about such via personal contact or on-the-turf research, that might be a good idea too.

EXPERIENCE: THE BEST TEACHER?

Experience shapes people, folk wisdom tells us. The question is, how, and to what degree?

It should be obvious enough that the life you lead is going to have a bearing on the person you ultimately become. If you've been a Charles Manson groupie or a resident of the New Mexico commune known as the Hog Farm, your point of view is unlikely ever to coincide with that of a deputy sheriff in rural Kansas. Growing up in the construction trades in Milwaukee seldom prepares you to think like a Yale professor of musicology or a Buddhist monk.

(Though you never can say for sure, you understand. Man's diversity is a major reason he intrigues us, and his flexibility, adaptability, and unpredictability is legendary. I once knew a longtime member of the Sailors Union of the Pacific who went on to become a certified public accountant, then changed gears to spread his wings as a leading mystery writer.)

What about what might be called shock impact—the kind of experience that so stuns as, allegedly, to turn a character's hair white overnight, or to induce lasting amnesia or paralysis or blindness?

Well, it does happen the psychiatrists tell us. The diagnosis frequently is one of conversion hysteria, and writers without number have used it as both a plot and character device. So many, in fact, that you can legitimately label it as overworked and so walk wide around it.

More realistically, will one traumatic event blight a life forever? Or can the victim rise above it? Do years of rigid discipline and conditioning erect so strong a wall that the person so trained can never escape it?

To ask such questions is to answer them. All of us have known far too many people who went their own way despite all pressures to the contrary. Carol Burnett overcame a childhood shared with alcoholic parents. Mary Higgins Clark suffered a series of traumatic losses in the deaths of those near and dear. Many Amish young people abandon the traditional life of their religion each year.

The issue, of course, is that no two of us respond to an experience, traumatic or otherwise, in precisely the same way. We each interpret each event that impinges on us in a highly individualized manner. I've known a number of cops who came out of the ghetto, including a few who had siblings in prison.

It's not the experience that creates the trauma, you see, but the way the character reacts to it. Insult one man, and he apologizes for existing. Another explodes in loud-mouthed anger. A third punches you in the nose. A fourth brushes off your insolence with a smile that hides his resolution that unpleasant things are going to happen to you in a darkened alley in the near future.

Generations of writers have taken advantage of this fact, and so should you. Indeed, that's why I talked about rationalization at such length in Chapter 2. It's the reason one person finds a joke hilarious, while another takes it as a wearisome bore. It's the key factor that makes one boy become a cop, his twin, a crook.

As a writer, you decide the impact of experience on your characters. Indeed, you devise experiences, incidents, to fit your story needs . . . then give them the meaning, to Character and to Reader, that you want them to have.

In a word, you *rationalize* each, precisely as described in Chapter 2.

What lies behind this strange anomaly? Quite possibly it's a vital, yet too often overlooked, constituent in the molding process that perhaps outweighs all the others. It's that of . . .

IDEAS: THE ULTIMATE CONDITIONERS

Too many years ago, in Depression days in Jackson, Michigan, the town where I grew up, I stumbled upon an informal organization that called itself the Thinkers Exchange.

Would that every boy might be as lucky! It reshaped my life.

The Exchange's membership was a disparate and unlikely group. It included, as I recall, a railroad fireman, a tool and die maker, a factory foreman, a blueprint technician, and a bicycle repairman. Lined faces, work-scarred hands, and broken nails were the order of the day. Virtually all those attending were self-educated. High school diplomas were a rarity. I doubt that a college degree ever darkened the group's conclaves.

Meeting once a month in a night-empty courtroom, the members mulled over topics ranging from events of the day to the meaning of the universe.

Yet the organization's name was no misnomer. Though limited as to background and formal education, and frequently arriving at what today seem strange conclusions indeed, these men were readers and thinkers, every one. Night after night, the shabby old courtroom vibrated with ideas. Here it was that I first heard of Charles Darwin and Michael Bakunin and Karl Marx. Clarence Meily's *Puritanism* and Paul Lafargue's *The Right to be Lazy* passed from hand to hand. The pros and cons of vaccination, vivisection, and euthanasia were debated fiercely. Fervent voices quoted Clarence Darrow and Margaret Sanger and Judge Ben Lindsay and Havelock Ellis and Robert G. Ingersoll. I found myself plunged into Morgan's *Ancient Society* and Ward's *The Ancient Lowly* and Kropotkin's *Mutual Aid as a Factor in Evolution.*

It was, I grant you, a unique situation. As I look back on it, I'm not at all sure that the years spent since in assorted colleges and universities contributed as much to my development.

So it is with ideas. Like body, environment, and experience, ideas shape both you and the characters about whom you write. It would be a mistake if you didn't consider such as you build your stories.

Also, as I hope I'm making clear, ideas don't spring just from books. People are far and away your greatest source and resource. Put yourself in contact with them every chance you get. Take advantage of their diversity to broaden your world, expand the limits of your own experience. Listen to them, talk with them, learn what they know and how they think and feel and reason.

I can't overemphasize the importance of this aspect of your development as a writer, as witness the case of a librarian under whom I worked for a time. Her story still fascinates me.

Librarian was the daughter of a wealthy, metropolitan banking family.

One day, Emma Goldman came to speak in Librarian's city.

This was the period just preceding World War I. Emma Goldman was a strident voice of militant anarchism, and of the radical feminism of the period.

For no reason beyond casual curiosity that I could ever ascertain, Librarian (who was a blighted socialite rather than a librarian at the time) went to hear Miss Goldman. And somehow, unfathomably, the things Emma Goldman said, the ideas she advanced with such fervor, struck a spark of social awareness within Librarian. Overnight, with new-convert zeal, she plunged into a tumultuous life of carrying the farther reaches of left-wing thought to the masses, on a level that soon had her in and out of jail on a well-nigh weekly basis.

Well, there's considerably more to Librarian's story, of course. But the thing that gripped and held me was the way an idea, the idea of anarchism (which I never could buy, incidentally, despite all Librarian's efforts to convert me) had transformed and reshaped a woman's life.

And mine also. Just knowing her, being fascinated by her, I found my own thinking about and insight into people expanded and given new facets and dimensions.

Nor are Librarian's case or mine isolated instances. Look around you at the people you know who have found new meaning in life through their contact with ideas, whether from print or people. Robert Heinlein's *Stranger in a Strange Land* influenced a whole generation, and so did Joseph Heller's *Catch 22,* and Jerry Falwell's preaching, and Timothy Leary's "drug revolution."

Or, if you feel I'm concentrating too much on the far-out fringes of our culture, consider the way that we grow up with such concepts as thrift or honesty or cynicism, progress or fate or kindliness or patriotism or devotion to duty conditioned into us.

Yes, ideas do count. You'll be shortchanging yourself and your characters alike if you don't bear them in mind when you create your story people. Let them think, let them believe, let them explore unique alleyways of opinion. Give them private concepts to ponder. Your stories will be the richer for it; your readers fascinated by the extra spice they offer.

Will the world accept such? Yes, if you don't allow the characters' attitudes to fall over the brink into propaganda. If you don't believe me, look over the mysteries of William Kienzle, whose major story people are Roman Catholic priests, or Harry Kemelman's series about a rabbi.

The insight and information these books give is, I believe, a major factor in making them best-sellers.

TYING IT ALL TOGETHER

Background can be summed up as "reasons why":

■ Reasons why a character does the things he does.
■ Reasons why he doesn't do others.

What's known as the "principle of parsimony" applies. That is, the simpler you can keep said reasons, the better. Which shouldn't be too difficult, since as writer, creator, you're in command. You simply rationalize the reasons.

Thus, as you prepare to write a story, most of the things you need to know about your characters will pop up automatically — by osmosis, as it were, through your skin, the way a frog takes in water. Only when they don't come do you need to sift through backgrounds in a systematic way.

When you do, simply ask yourself such questions as are needed — and only such; after all, you're writing a story, not working through research for a doctoral dissertation.

So, ask questions —

■ Does anything about this character's *body* have a bearing on his feeling, his thinking, his behavior, within the story framework?
■ How about his *environment*?
■ His *experience*?
■ His *ideas*?

Keep at it, and believe me, you'll get answers to solve your problems.

One word of warning, though: The degree to and manner in which you develop characters depends on the kind of story you're writing and the audience for which you're writing it.

While this is a point we'll discuss in more detail in Chapters 10 and 14, it should do no harm to warn you here that an action thriller ordinarily requires less depth and detail in regard to character than does a literary story.

But all this is extraneous to another issue which calls for immediate attention: how to create far-out story people when and if you need them.

We'll explore the subject in "Wild Cards," our next chapter.

9

WILD CARDS

*What goes into building an
offbeat character?
The same elements that you use in
creating any story person —
only more so.*

A wild card, in poker, is one that may be played as any value the player wishes to assign it. Thus, a "wild" trey may be played as an ace, a jack, a seven, or anything else the player who holds it needs.

When you're writing a story, you sometimes need a character like that — one who doesn't fit the norm, the pattern of accepted values. A wild card, as it were. An individual who's so far out and off the beaten track that he gives you a manipulative edge as needed.

Judging by the standards to which most of us adhere, virtually all such offbeat characters march to the storied different drummer. Specifically, we see key aspects of their behavior as *irrational* — warped, distorted, illogical, deviant. Which is to say, some such characters are, at the very least, eccentrics. Others, even farther out, are those colloquially dubbed psychos.

How do you create such a character?

The procedure is the same as for developing any other story person. You label him with a dominant impression . . . flesh him out with tags and traits . . . assign him an appropriate rationale as needed in terms of purpose, motive, and background.

There are, however, a few caveats to bear in mind . . . chugholes and pitfalls you should be aware of. They're the topic of this chapter.

First of all, what about . . .

THE ECCENTRICS

My dictionary says that an eccentric is someone who deviates from accepted usage or conduct.

"The true eccentric," says Carl Sifakis in his *American Eccentrics,* "follows his own rules of behavior twenty-four hours a day — because he knows his code is the right one and everyone else is wrong; because he does not want to compete by conventional standards; or because eccentricity seems the only way to gain recognition as an individual. Even among the super-rich, there are those who turn to the outrageous in their desire not to be considered just another millionaire."

It's a definition that covers a lot of ground. It has to, if it's to include Hetty Green, the miserly "Witch of Wall Street," a millionairess who saved soap by washing only the bottom inches of her long black skirts . . . John Symmes, a retired infantry captain who spent years trying to persuade Congress that Earth was a hollow ball, which could be entered via a hole at the North Pole . . . James Eads, the "millionaire hobo" who nearly starved to death when he refused to spend inherited money because he hadn't earned it . . . Ferdinand Demara, the "Great Imposter," a high school dropout who passed himself off as a Canadian naval surgeon, a Trappist monk, a college teacher, and a prison guidance counselor . . . and Lillie Coit (for whom San Francisco's Coit Tower is named), socialite beauty and the Knickerbocker Engine Company's fire buff supreme.

Eccentrics and eccentricity are valuable to a writer because, being out of skew from the accepted pattern of behavior, by their difference and uniqueness, frequently they create reader interest beyond that generated by the ordinary run of characters.

Such deviations from the norm are, obviously, a matter of degree. They can range from your friend who's bothered if he steps on a crack in the sidewalk, to the individual who wears a top hat and scarlet-lined opera cape every day, to the monomaniac who tries to strike up a conversation on the evils of water fluoridation with anyone he meets. Agatha Christie's books are full of them, and so are those of Martha Grimes, Gary Jennings, and Stephen King.

And that's not even to mention Shakespeare, Dickens, Trollope, or Stevenson.

What makes an eccentric? A variety of factors, of course. Ordinarily, it seems to me, he's someone who, consciously or unconsciously, feels a tremendous need to maintain his individuality. To that end, he has selected some limited aspect of life and living in which he holds unbendingly to his private standards. His whim is the Gibraltar to which he clings and on which he has erected his entire personality structure. In some respects, in all likelihood, he's obsessive-compulsive, as in the case of our sidewalk crack-avoider. In others, he quite possibly is schizoid—a loner, shy and unsociable, who has focused on some narrow vein of interest well-nigh to the point of paranoia.

In any event, ordinarily he's looked upon as an oddball—"different." His preoccupation with his warp or obsession, the tenacity with which he clings to it, at once sets him apart and calls attention to him. You can see the result portrayed in Rex Stout's obese, orchid-loving detective, Nero Wolfe. Sherlock Holmes, too, qualifies. So does Auntie Mame. And Frank Baum's *The Wizard of Oz* is a gold mine of the eccentric's characteristic narrow focus: the Scarecrow, searching for a brain; the Cowardly Lion, seeking courage; the Tin Woodman, wanting a heart; and the Wizard himself, maintaining ego by perpetuation of a fraud.

As a first step in developing such a character, you need to ask yourself three questions:

1. What form does Eccentric's eccentricity take?
2. What purpose does it serve for him?
3. How do you want readers to feel about him?

Let's consider these points one at a time, even though they clearly are interpendent in most cases.

Where Question 1 is concerned, the issue is what Eccentric says or does that shows that he's eccentric. Simply labeling him a queer duck isn't enough. You need to let him arrange his currency by serial number in his wallet, or always speak in verse, or wear earmuffs in August if he's to convince your audience he really is peculiar. (Yes, I know I'm exaggerating, but bear with me.) Indeed, it might even be to your advantage to keep an eye out for usable quirks and twists as you go about your daily routine. A list of such may later come in handy.

On to Question 2: What purpose does Eccentric's behavior serve for him? Or, to phrase it another way, what does Eccentric hope to gain by his peculiarities, his offbeat lifestyle?

This is a matter of major consequence, believe me. A potentially disastrous fault of unthinking writers is their tendency simply to saddle an eccentric character with far-out nuttiness, with no consideration for logic or whether or not his behavior adds up to anything meaningful within the story framework or anywhere else. Since the casual observer can detect no perceptible pattern in Eccentric's actions, he assumes none exists.

Actually, of course, eccentrics do have reasons for doing the things they do, even though they may have forgotten them years ago. And once you decide on a reason for the behavior of your particular eccentric, your character—for your own private use in planning, if nothing else—your story will make a great deal more sense, as well as ease your task as a writer.

But if an eccentric doesn't know why he acts as he does, how can you expect to?

The answer, naturally enough, is that you can't. But your tool for coping with the situation is close at hand and, by this time, should be ever so familiar.

That is, you *rationalize* an appropriate reason for whatever happens. Putting the serial numbers on dollar bills in order becomes the hallmark of a personality distorted by super-caution, twisted residue of a mother's tears on rent day when her purse was pilfered. Earmuffs in August may represent an effort to shut out inner voices that berate him.

Why bother with such backing and filling? Because it helps you to keep Eccentric's conduct consistent. Awareness that this story person is a bit off center where money matters are concerned, and why, will open all sorts of possibilities for you as the pages pile up. Whereas only confusion will result if, on one page, he's driving his friends and neighbors up the wall with diatribes on the metric system as a communist plot, while the next page sees him racked by a deep-seated fear that his brother will loose mind-things from another world to plague him.

Question 3: How do you want readers to feel about Eccentric? Is your goal for them to like him? Dislike him? Accept him? Reject him? React to him with amusement? Scorn? Disgust? Pity?

The importance of these questions should be on the obvious side. They make the difference between thrifty and stingy, considerate and weak, firm and brutal. The answers you decide upon will determine the kind of incidents in which you involve your particular eccentric—the specific bits of action and business and color you devise to show him to best advantage to get the audience reaction you desire. It will be difficult for readers to feel much kinship for the woman who pulses rank body odors because she feels that bathing reduces her resistance to disease, or to listen with much patience to the man who monopolizes conversation with dire warnings of an impending invasion by earthworms. And, on the flip side, who can grow too upset with the elderly lady who talks to her cats or insists on dressing in the styles of 1925?

It's an area in which the catch-as-catch-can approach is a frail reed indeed to rely upon. Thought and pre-planning will serve you better.

THE PSYCHOS

In its most common usage, the term *psycho* means any person suffering from a psychosis or major neurosis—that is to say, a more or less severe emotional illness.

The fiction writer, however, seldom is dealing with precise clinical categories. His concern is with the practical problems of how his "wild cards" may best be played in his stories.

It's also a fact that the line between the eccentric and the psycho can be thin to the point of nonexistence, the degree of deviance from the norm ranging from minor peculiarities of behavior to disruptions of personality so severe as to require continuing medication or confinement on the back ward of a mental hospital. Cases in point extend from Colin Wilson's *Ritual in the Dark* and Ken Kesey's *One Flew over the Cuckoo's Nest* to the low IQ of Lenny in John Steinbeck's *Of Mice and Men* and the fragile psyche of Blanche in Tennessee Williams's *A Streetcar Named Desire*.

In practical terms, one of the most useful approaches may be to say that the eccentric tends to be open in his aberration and viewed as harmless, while the psycho masks his or is mistrusted or feared.

The basis for this distinction lies in the fact that, by and large for most people, eccentric equates with harmless, psycho with menace. Ashley "Ash the Flash" Cripps, an eccentric in Martha Grimes's *The Anodyne Necklace*, is openly following his own road in terms of exhibitionism in womens restrooms. In *Psycho*, however, Norman Bates keeps his murderous impulses hidden, even though his quarters indicate that he's hardly the usual motel owner.

A few cameos may help to sharpen the picture.

Our character, Elaine, is an upwardly mobile woman. Young,

good looking, highly competent in her field, she's clearly cut out for success.

Except for one thing.

She drinks.

Other people in her circle have noticed it, of course. She knows it. It terrifies her, for she's sharply, bitterly aware that the next step will make it apparent in the workplace too. Once that happens, the road she's traveling will lead down, not up.

Why doesn't she stop? She doesn't know, can't figure it out. Or, to put it another way, her behavior is *irrational*.

Consider another character—a man, this time: Ralph Jastrow.

Shyness is Ralph's problem. Drop him into any kind of social situation, any circumstance that involves interacting with people, and he freezes. This is bad enough where social affairs are concerned. At business conferences it becomes disastrous. Yet though it makes Ralph miserable, there seems to be nothing he can do about it. Sometimes he's thought of seeking professional help. But he finds he's too shy to make the appointment—and that's irrational, to say the least.

Yet Ralph's dilemma is trivial compared with that of one of his acquaintances, Stanley Horton.

Stanley has a thing about little boys. He's drawn to them so strongly that his life has come to revolve around them. He teaches a Sunday School class, leads a Boy Scout troop, serves as buddy and confidante to every kid on the block. Indeed, it amuses (and upon occasion irritates) his wife; she says he's closer to the youngsters than he is to her.

Unfortunately, that's only the beginning. Because the secret games Stanley plays with the boys he knows best involve penitentiary offenses. If his wife were aware of them—well, that would be even worse than prison; Stanley already has made up his mind to kill himself at the first hint that the horrifying skeleton in his closet has been discovered. If he could bring himself to talk about his situation, he'd be the first to agree that the whole weird phantasmagoria of his world is, to say the least, irrational.

Then there's Anna, who can't stop talking. Gretchen, who always takes a small "gift" or two with her when she leaves a store. Dave, at the bank, with the tic that makes him grimace and blink as he works. Dr. Morris, the psychiatrist who's compulsive to the point that he scrambles to retrieve any paper that falls to the floor during a therapy session. Cora, so grossly fat her husband swears he's going to leave her. Austin, the hermit of Maple Street, hiding in his crumbling Victorian home like one of the Collyer brothers, New York's famed recluse of another day.

Wild cards, all of them. Men and women who somehow walk a different road than their fellows as they move through life, trapped in a maze of irrational behavior despite all their efforts to escape it.

As with the eccentric, three questions will help to guide you through the labyrinth that is the psycho:

1. What does Psycho do that reveals his deviance?
2. How does he mask it from his fellows?
3. What logic lies behind his madness?

Which brings up a related question only you can answer: Do you limit yourself to objective reporting in dealing with the psycho, or is it to your advantage to enter his mind?

A case can be made for either side. On the one hand, the more you can wrap your deviant in a mantle of mystery, the better your chance of bringing him off. On the other hand, tell the story—or part of it—from his viewpoint so we know what he's thinking, and your readers may end up understanding and sympathizing with him. For as the old adage has it, "To know all is to forgive all."

I can recall an old story of my own that drew much of its strength, I was told, from the fact that alternate chapters were written in the viewpoint of the villain—he was known only as "The Murderer" until the very last scene—and revealed his thoughts and feelings as well as his actions.

Perhaps the best way out is to experiment, trying both techniques and then selecting the one that seems most effective for that particular story.

You also need at least a bit of insight into why the psycho behaves as he does. What turns him to irrational action?

As a starting point, we must put irrationality itself under the microscope . . . ask ourselves just what constitutes such behavior.

For our purposes here, let's define it as action that sees a character doing something he knows better than.

"Knows better than" means "would know better than, *if Character were normal*."

This perhaps will come through more clearly if I remind you that most of the characters we write about conform to society's standards, by and large . . . adapt themselves to the demands that group life places on them. The viewpoint character, in particular, is almost always rational. Stupidity of consequence on his part tends to be limited to comedic situations. Or at least he can always make excuses for himself and his behavior.

Or, look in a mirror. You can always justify your actions to yourself, can't you? Even when you disapprove of said actions?

In a wild card character's viewpoint, however, the situation's different. Because your story person is irrational in his thinking, which means you have to deal with someone who's convinced that his sister is poisoning him, or that the man next door is projecting slanderous radio waves into his head, or that the world is coming to an end at 9:00 A.M. tomorrow.

You must then devise ways to show that irrationality, through viewpoint insights—looking into Character's head and revealing what he's thinking—or objectively, via Character's dialogue or behavior, as when the nephew in *Arsenic and Old Lace,* who has the delusion he's Teddy Roosevelt, lunges up the stairs, shouting "Charge!"

Bear in mind, too, that intellectually the wild card may be perfectly well aware that he's acting in a socially unacceptable manner and against his own best interests.

Or his behavior may seem entirely logical to him. Or, even if he recognizes that it makes no sense, he may be at a loss to control the impulse. Robert Louis Stevenson's *Dr. Jekyll and Mr. Hyde,* in which Dr. Jekyll loses control of himself to his drug-induced alter ego, Mr. Hyde, offers the classic example.

In any case, he goes right on doing whatever it is he's doing. Why? Call it, if you will, a situation in which tension has built up to a point where emotion so overloads intellect as to bring on a loss of rational control.

How does such an emotional overload work? One way to explain it would be to say that in each of our lives various factors exist that create tension.

We find these elements disturbing, upsetting. Inordinately so, in some of us. Yet because they're so upsetting, we find it difficult to face them, meet them head on, deal with them in a rational— which is to say, intelligent, realistic—manner.

Bottled up, carried to extremes, the tensions such elements create can be painful—emotionally distressing, the way a guilty conscience or an unrequited love or an undissipated grief or a dreadful disappointment would be distressing if projected to the *n*th degree.

In an effort to evade this pain, this tension we somehow can't release, we attempt on an unconscious level to dodge around the issue, whatever it is.

We do this, the psychologists say, by means of various mental mechanisms, techniques of evasion. Displacement (an attack against a person or object less dangerous than the one that's upsetting you—you don't dare kick the boss, so you kick the dog or yell at your wife) probably is the most common, though there are a wide assortment of others: progression, fixation, conversion, regression, dissociation, and so on; see your library's books on psychiatry or psychology for details.

Thus, Elaine escapes from her "upwardly mobile" strains in a bottle. Ralph walks wide around his fear of people via shyness. Stanley becomes a child molester. Anna strives to lower her tension level with endless babblings. Gretchen turns to shoplifting, kleptomania. Dave develops a tic, an involuntary, nervous twitching. Dr. Morris succumbs to obsessive-compulsive tendencies to neatness. Cora calms uneasiness with food. Austin, as a recluse, shuts out the world.

Such tendencies, to a degree, are present in all of us. I try to slough off confrontational phone calls. My wife is uneasy if dirty dishes stand on the sinkboard overnight. My neighbor detests dogs and children. So long as such quirks don't get out of hand, who cares? It's ordinarily a matter of little consequence whether we can figure out or otherwise unearth the origins of such feelings. Odds are our second-guessings would prove wrong in any case.

(Unless we need an angle for story purposes, that is. In which circumstance, the answer of course is the one set forth in Chapter 8: Assign an appropriate cause arbitrarily, and then rationalize it.)

What *does* matter is that you recognize that not every aspect of character in a story need be neatly wrapped and packaged. Better by far that you face up to the vagaries of human nature, the "wild card" aspects of character set forth in this chapter. Certainly it will add color, realism, and interest to your story people, and your readers will love you for it.

A character with a "wild card" twist may of course pop up in a story whether you will it or no — a sudden flash of inspiration that solves a problem, or strikes a needed note of tension, or shows potentialities for developing a new plot thread. If that happens, I trust that this chapter will show you how to deal with him or her.

Which doesn't mean you *have* to introduce such people, you understand. In most stories you'll neither need or want them. But when you encounter a situation in which you need a character whose behavior is incomprehensible or irrationally out of line with most people's view of the world, an eccentric or psycho may be the answer. Just be careful that you know *why* you've chosen to use him or her, in terms of your plot, and that you're fully aware of how to create and handle the individual.

It may help if you are aware of the things a psychiatrist looks for when he's trying to decide whether or not a person is "sane" (whatever that means; it's a subject on which there's anything but total agreement, as witness the dissenting views of such insightful specialists as Thomas Szasz, E. Fuller Torrey, and R. D. Laing).

The first step, obviously, is observation. Check out the people with whom you come in contact who strike you as behaving irrationally — that is, acting in a manner they "know better than." Note the things they do that set them aside and betray a warp in judgment.

Appearance will play a considerable role. A man who persists in wearing a woman's bra over his shirt is likely to rouse speculation. So will a woman who shaves a broad strip the length of her head, or cuts away her dress so one breast hangs bare.

Indeed, *changes* in appearance will be remarked. If I have been known for neatness all my adult life, then start coming to social affairs and church unshaven and in dirty shirt and torn sweater, people will begin to look askance.

Behavior, too, will play a role. When, one night at choir practice, I suddenly lift my skirt crotch-high and sing and dance in a most unbecoming manner, it will attract attention. Same for wandering through backyards at night, becoming lost on my way to the grocery store, or making garbled phone calls to the police and FBI.

More subtle, less easily detected, are inner twists and changes. And indeed, for the writer, there's little need to heed them until they manifest themselves outwardly. Charles Whitman, the Texas Tower killer, offers a case in point. He appeared perfectly normal, a model young man, until he gunned down sixteen innocent victims.

Finally, it's important to probe self-insight. "Why are you here? What's bothering you? What seems to be your problem?" are questions every therapist must ask, sooner or later.

An additional item to remember as you build your story people is a comment by Dr. John Duval Campbell in his *Everyday Psychiatry:*

> . . . *one personality type does not change into another personality type . . . If the patient has a psychoneurotic makeup today he will have a psychoneurotic constitution a year from now or even 20 years from now . . . A schizoid personality remains schizoid throughout life, and a psychopathic personality remains a psychopath. A schizoid does not become a psychoneurotic, and a psychoneurotic does not change, regardless of what the stress may be, into a hypomanic or mental defective. This immutability of personality types is the most useful and dependable law the beginner can learn in psychiatry.*

What is the significance of this observation for the writer?

First, it's a warning against labeling any character of consequence as simply "crazy." To do so is to expose your ignorance at an embarrassing level.

Second, it tells you how important it is that you do enough research on any "wild card" character so you can decide intelligently what kind of problem he has and provide him with appropriate symptoms to carry off the role.

Do understand, I'm not proposing that you earn your doctorate in clinical psychology before you start to write. Scanning a book or two probably will familiarize you with the field enough to prevent your going too far overboard. Indeed, beware of delving too deeply into research, for such can become a trap that has you forever studying instead of writing. Make your motto, "Write first; correct later." It really does work better that way!

(Unless you're proposing to write psychological or pseudo-psychological novels like Robert L. Duncan's *The Serpent's Mark* or Terry Cline's *Missing Persons* or Thomas Harris's *Red Dragon*, that is. If that's your yen you can hardly do too much digging.

One final question: what about using the eccentric or psycho as a viewpoint character?

Well, it can be done, certainly. Witness Poe's "The Tell-Tale Heart" and Alfred Bester's *The Demolished Man* and Fredric Brown's *Knock Three-One-Two* and Robert Bloch's *The Scarf*—not to mention various of Stephen King's assorted strolls through nightmare. It's not necessarily easy, though, and many readers find such tales distasteful.

Further, horror—that's the category into which psycho-view-point novels tend to fall—has become pretty much a specialty, so you need to be thoroughly familiar with the genre if you're to avoid the stereotypes that bring rejection.

But you'll work that out on your own. Right now, it's time to turn to another aspect of the fictioneer's craft that of necessity is important to every writer: the task of dealing with special problems that revolve around building the different characters found in virtually every story.

You'll find some ideas on the subject in the next chapter: "The Role of Roles."

10

THE ROLE OF ROLES

*How do you treat a hero?
You shape the hero to fit the job he or
she has to do.*

In each story you write there'll be certain characters who, by virtue of special attributes they possess or the roles they play, warrant special attention.

We'll consider some of those characters in this chapter. Specifically, let's turn the spotlight on:

- The interesting character
- The memorable character
- The viewpoint character
- The protagonist
- The antagonist
- The love interest character
- The incidental character
- The non-human character

Let's consider characters with special attributes first, bearing in mind always that said attributes are by no means limited to particular story people. To greater or less degree, the things I say about them will apply to every member of your cast. By isolating the discussion of each category here, the principles involved will stand out more sharply.

THE INTERESTING CHARACTER

Yes, every character you write about should be interesting, and in all likelihood will be. But if one or more seem to have the blahs, here are the tools you need to remedy the situation.

First off, the key fact to remember is that the dull character ordinarily is the predictable character—the one who always reacts in the same way, as when Hero is always noble and Heroine is always virtuous and Villain always fiendish.

How to overcome this? Provide the character with logical yet unanticipated aspects of personality, so that Reader can no longer take Character's behavior and reactions for granted.

Thus, Hero may be noble. But perhaps he also holds opinions that take readers aback. Example: the downgrading of the importance of rape by series hero Matt Helm in one of Donald Hamilton's novels. Or a straight arrow hero, believing the end justifies the means, may treat an opponent with brutal cruelty in order to get information.

Heroine, in turn, is the soul of honesty. Yet when she taps the till for a worthy cause, telling herself she'll return the money when she draws her next pay, your audience will look at her with new eyes, wondering if perhaps she'll dip in again the next time round. And fiendish Villain quite possibly has a thing about kittens that leads him to croon to and cuddle a stray as if it were a long-lost child.

Tony Hillerman's Navajo policemen frequently draw reader attention by behaving in an unpredictable manner—unpredictable to a non-Navajo, that is. Hillerman always explains the Indian custom which renders such behavior believable. But in the meantime he's captured audience attention.

Nan Hamilton deviated from the standard detective when she introduced Ohara, a Japanese officer who meditates as well as captures criminals.

Ethnic characters often are made interesting by virtue of such handling. Their actions and attitudes vary from that expected by the public.

This kind of thing can operate on any level. Sherlock Holmes and his cocaine offer a prime example. And I recall one of my own stories in which I gave a cold-eyed gambler in the pioneer West a sentimental streak, quite in contrast to the other elements of his personality. It not only helped distinguish him from stereotypical gamblers featured in the western pulps; it made him more interesting and, in the resolution, was paid off when he spent his last twenty-dollar gold piece on a doll for a little girl.

THE MEMORABLE CHARACTER

It might be nice if one way or another you made your hero or heroine—and perhaps assorted other characters—unique, memorable. For although this can be overdone, few things are more likely to prove fatal to a story than the passive character, the forgettable character, the character who fades into the woodwork.

On the other hand, readers are hardly likely to forget Jack Bickham's Wildcat O'Shea, who rode the range through more than a dozen volumes in a, shall we say, colorful costume:

> *Coming up the road from the left, heading toward town, was a giant roan. Slouching in the saddle with a blue Stetson pulled brim-out around his head was a tall, wide-shouldered, long-legged gent. His saddle fenders were painted crimson and Mexican silver work glittered. He wore with the blue hat a green shirt and purple vest, a yellow belt, orange pants and boots that had been painted lavender. A huge Colt hung down his right hip, in a silvery holster. He had two shell belts crossed over his chest, and a carbine slung over his back, and out of the bedroll tied on the horse's rump stuck two cylindrical objects, one of which had to be the neck of a bottle and the other of which looked chillingly like a stick of dynamite. The man was just riding along, bouncing with the horse, yet even in his careless slouch he managed to convey a sense of lazy grace over the distance.*

The same holds true for the woman in Michael Avallone's first Ed Noon novel, *The Tall Dolores*:

> *I'll begin by telling you she was the tallest girl that ever came into my office. But tall isn't the word for it. Not really. As spotty as my schooling was, I can do better than that.*
>
> *Dolores was a hell of a lot more than tall. She was huge, statuesque. A Glamazon. A regular Empire State Building of female feminine dame. And all woman besides.*
>
> *Six feet three in her stocking feet. Don't scoff. Don't laugh at the notion. Don't even faint. Put black pumps with three-inch heels on those feet and you'll get a rough sketch of the shadow she threw across my threshold the day she crossed it.*

Not that such physical uniqueness is necessarily a requirement for a memorable character. Aaron Elkin's Gideon Oliver is distinguished by his unusual occupation as a forensic anthropologist, dubbed the "skeleton detective." Frank Gruber delighted an audience with his human encyclopedia, Oliver Quade. John Le Carré reverses the glamour image of secret agents to hook readers with the dull gray realism of George Smiley, antithesis of Ian Fleming's flamboyant James Bond.

Even minor characters can be given color with minimal wordage. Witness Father Budreau, a priest in William X. Kienzle's *Assault with Intent*, who carries a derringer along with his rosary. Or "Ash the Flash" in Martha Grimes's *The Anodyne Necklace*, with his long track record of exposing himself in women's restrooms.

For the ultimate memorable character, and a minor character at that, I nominate Checkers Chauncey, presented by Joe Lansdale in *The Magic Wagon*.

> *He was a nose picker, and about the best I've ever seen at it. He didn't do it like a lady will do, like she ain't really doing it, but just scratching, and her finger will shoot in and scoop out the prize and she'll flick it away before you can say, "Hey, ain't that a booger?"*
>
> *He didn't even do it like some men do, which is honest, but not unpolite. They'll turn sort of to the side and get in there after it in a businesslike manner, but you didn't actually have to witness the work or what come of it.*
>
> *No. Checkers Chauncey, who I think of as Nose Picker Chauncey, must have once been a miner or a mule whacker, as they're the nastiest, and most mannerless creatures on earth. There ain't a thing they won't do in front of man, child, or lady. They just don't give a damn. Chauncey went about his digging front-on and open, using his finger so hard it rose a mound on his nostrils, like a busy groundhog throwing up dirt. And when he got what he was looking for, he always held it in front of him just to see, I guess, if he'd accidentally found something other than what he'd expected, and when he thumped it away you had to be kind of fast on your feet, because he didn't care who or what it stuck to.*

So much for Chauncey. Even if you find him disgusting or distasteful, one thing's for certain, I guarantee you. You won't forget him!

How do you create a memorable character? Focus, it seems to me, is the key factor. *Your* focus.

That is, you select some unique aspect of body, mind, background, or personality in your story person, then emphasize it. Build it up. Exaggerate it. Make it striking and colorful enough that *you* remember it, the way you remember Nero Wolfe's weight or Quasimodo's hump or Auntie Mame's wild spontaneity or Mr. Spock's lack of emotion or Pollyanna's optimism and tendency to find good in everything.

Then, in the words of Lester Dent, creator of Doc Savage, wave those tags! Bring them in over and over again, so that your readers have no opportunity to forget them and the character they represent. Whereupon, before you know it, you just may have created a striking, memorable story person.

One final item: The examples I've chosen above are super-broadbrush, wildly exaggerated where many markets are concerned. I've picked them intentionally in order to make my point. I assume, however, that you have judgment enough to temper the concept to fit your own tastes and story.

THE VIEWPOINT CHARACTER

Whatever your story, your readers will need some kind of orientation point, some place from which to watch the action. In other words, a *point* of view.

Ordinarily that "point" is in a character—a viewpoint character. Or, as I used to put it, "Whose skin are we in?" Through whose eyes are we seeing or experiencing the story?

In choosing this character, you limit yourself to presenting your story as he experiences it. That is to say, he can watch what other story people do, but he can't see himself.

He will, however, know anything you want your readers to know about his own state of mind:

"Damn you, Jack Dalton!" he choked. But that was as far as he dared go. Dalton's hand already was on the gun. One wrong move on his own part and he'd be dead.

You want to show Character in action from the outside? Then

switch to another viewpoint character—an observer, like Doctor Watson worshipfully watching Sherlock Holmes perform his miracles of deduction. Here's what Dalton sees:

> *Slade's face turned scarlet. His nostrils flared. He bared his teeth in a savage, death's-head grin.*

Only from the outside can we see the color of Slade's face, or the flaring of his nostrils, or the death's-head grin.

This can be very effective, but by and large it's limited in emotional intensity. And the interpretation of what's happening is strictly Observer's, and not necessarily correct. Looking at Character from the outside, readers won't know what he thinks or feels or sees save as it's translated into appearance or action. Is he angry? You can't say so, because you're *outside* him and therefore don't know what he's feeling or thinking unless he turns red in the face, clenches his fists, and cries, "Damn you, Jack Dalton!" or equivalent. And even then you can't be sure the feeling he exhibits isn't faked.

A third alternative is to jump around in the story like a frog on a hot griddle. One moment, the presentation may be objective, with the author reporting, interpreting, explaining. The next, quite possibly, it hops in and out of the hearts and minds of an assortment of characters when it suits the author's whim.

This is what's known as *author omniscient* viewpoint.

Here, an example from John D. MacDonald's *Please Write for Details,* a general novel rather than his usual suspense:

> *They were the girls of Texas, Mary Jane—twenty, Bitsy, nineteen, leggy and brown and arrogant and derisive of everything in the world including themselves. They wore very short shorts and very narrow halters and, at stops during the trip down, had come dangerously close to causing a civil riot and insurrection.*

This, of course, is reporting that is objective in form, but that is actually ever so subjective because it involves selection and interpretation of details to the author's taste.

There's more of this alleged objective approach, a great deal more, in which MacDonald explains and analyzes the two girls and the book's other characters on a variety of levels. But eventually he goes *inside* — that is, into the viewpoint of — a character, Miles Drummond.

> *Miles trotted out to the dining room after it was dark to look at the tables and* **worry** *about the seating.*

I emphasize the **worry** because it's a feeling and only Miles can know that it exists. Which means that, temporarily at least, we're in Miles's viewpoint.

Later,

> *. . . The light filled the room with eerie shadows and left the high ceiling in darkness. He got a chair and removed the shades and then stepped back to look it over. It was worse without the shades. He replaced them. The place settings distressed him. He liked things to be very nice. He hoped that the light was so dim that they would not notice the dozen breeds and brands of glasses, silver and china, or the dim stains and mends and worn spots in the tableclothes . . .*

And so on. Further, this is more than just description. The things Miles notices and the way he reacts to them characterize him, make him very much an individual human being with tastes and standards and feelings.

As the story progresses, we move into other viewpoints:

> *John Kemp felt unduly pleased that the luck of the draw had put him beside Barbara Kilmer, but that advantage was canceled out by Gam Torrigan being seated on her left . . .*

Again,

> *Agnes Partridge Keeley felt curiously isolated from the group. At her left . . .*

Back to Miles again:

> *Miles thought the food tasted a bit strange, and he looked*

*up and down the table . . . He made a mental note to talk
to Margarita and Esperanza about serving. It was unnecessary to bang things down so briskly.*

And so it goes as MacDonald moves us skillfully from character
to character, building each into an individual with private quirks
and tastes and goals.

Let me point out, too, my use of that word "skillfully" in the
paragraph above. For because MacDonald has skill born of long
experience, he can handle author omniscient with an ability most
of us lack.

Because "author omniscient" flits from character to character
pretty much sans pattern, it both tends to prove confusing and to
lack the emotional impact that comes from living through the story
with a single (or possibly two or three) highly involved people. At
the very least, ordinarily, it should stay with a character for a chapter at a time. Otherwise the cost frequently is higher than the return.

What about the technique of telling the story entirely from
outside any character — the objective, "I Am A Camera" approach?

Well, obviously, it can be done. Hammett became famous for
it in *The Maltese Falcon.*

Again, however, the issue is skill. Can you create feeling and
emotion in a character, and for readers, without going inside his
head? If you can, fine, but for most of us it isn't nearly as effective
as presenting our story in terms of a subjectively oriented central
figure.

Most fiction today uses this technique. It focuses on and re-
solves around a viewpoint character who's the chief sufferer, the
individual who's most involved emotionally and who has the most
to win or lose. It presents the story from *inside* this character —
letting the readers see what Character sees, hear what Character
hears, taste/smell/touch/think/feel what Character does. In a word,
readers *experience* the story, *live through it,* with the viewpoint
character, and thus receive maximum emotional impact and satis-
faction.

Choosing the right viewpoint is vitally important. Suppose, for
example, that you have a story that centers on high school football.
Three of the major characters are the star running back, the coach,
and the running back's girlfriend. Colored by his or her own feel-

ings and desires, each sees the situation differently. Which should you choose as viewpoint?

Let's look at a fragment of a game as each experiences it.

First, the player, the running back:

> *As if somehow frozen in time, slowly, slowly, the pigskin spiralled down. Desperately, Steve raced to intercept it . . . poised beneath it, heart pounding and standing still at once. Nail this pass and he'd have it made—the play, the game, the championship. And Vonya.*

The boldface italics mark Steve's viewpoint. Only he, the viewpoint character, could know what's in his heart and mind at this moment.

Second, the coach:

> *Atkins' fists clenched so tight they ached. He couldn't get breath into his lungs. If that damn ox Steve tripped over his feet again, missed this one—*

Do you see the pattern? Only Atkins can know that his fists ache or that he can't get breath into his lungs, let alone know his thoughts about Steve.

Finally, Vonya:

> *Vonya hung suspended in an awful, downward spiral like the ball. Steve mustn't catch it! He mustn't! Not when she'd already promised Tony about tonight.*

Vonya's thoughts, Vonya's feelings. Her emotional reactions to the situation. That's what constitutes viewpoint. And as you see, each individual has his own.

Above and beyond that, if you're limited to one of these story people's viewpoints, which will you pick to tell your tale? Which will be most effective? Which will prove most gripping for your readers?

I can give you no answer, of course. The decision, ever and always, must be yours. It will depend on your decisions, your insights, the story you want to tell. All I can do is warn you to make your decision carefully, looking at the problem from all angles.

Because it's one of the most important choices you can make.

It will help, however, if you remember five things where your viewpoint character is concerned.

First, it's through the viewpoint character that you orient your readers to a story, let them know whose story it is.

Second, being inside somebody's skin is a major way — maybe *the* major way — to grip your readers. It provides instant identification and empathy with the character.

Third, once you're inside somebody's skin — that is, in viewpoint — you can't legitimately enter another character's mind. You can show him only in terms of externals, what he says and does.

Fourth, a viewpoint character can't lie about his inner feelings. The reader is *inside* the character, so what the character feels or thinks or sees or whatever, the reader knows about. Which means that if Character is a con man, you can't edit the fact that he's trying to marry Heroine for her money from his thoughts.

(Do you want to keep your readers guessing? Then don't go inside the character's head.)

Fifth, your audience in all likelihood will be a key factor in your choice of viewpoint. In our Steve-Coach-Vonya specimen, for example, Steve will probably be the viewpoint character if the story's aimed at a teen sports magazine. A girl's magazine? Vonya. A sports or service magazine? Quite possibly Coach Atkins.

Beyond this, you as writer have a whole series of additional choices to make.

Thus, whatever Character's position, whether as protagonist or observer, this individual, this viewpoint character, may be presented in first person ("I") or third person ("he"/"she") or, on rare occasions, second person ("you"). It's a matter of personal choice.

First person offers a level of intimacy and insight that's very effective. To a considerable degree, however, it puts a straightjacket on the writer, for it also limits the scope of presentation to what the "I" storyteller can observe and makes it awkward to change viewpoint. Some readers and some editors loathe it. But it's overwhelmingly popular with others, and thousands of short stories and novels using it have been published.

Third person, in contrast, tells the story "he/she," as a participant observer might. Ordinarily that observer is one of the characters. Its weakness lies in the fact that it prevents the viewpoint character from seeing himself in action. By and large, it means that you can't describe Character's appearance save as other characters see him.

Second person? It tells the story as "you" experience it. The best example of it with which I'm acquainted is Ralph Milney Farley's "The House of Ecstasy," and its very rarity as a technique is proof of the difficulty of managing it effectively. I'd class it as a *tour de force* and not worth bothering with except as an experiment.

What about having more than one viewpoint? It's legitimate enough, certainly—I recall at least one suspense novel where the author had a different first-person viewpoint character for each of twenty chapters, heaven help me! And to have two or three viewpoints is not at all unusual.

Remember, though, that viewpoint switches may be confusing and hard to handle. It takes space to establish each viewpoint—and in a short story you seldom have that much wordage to squander. In consequence, multiple viewpoint tends to be limited to the longer forms.

Yet a change in viewpoint allows you to introduce information known to or experienced by the new character, and that's a plus. In a suspense novel, for example, a switch to what my friend Jack Bickham refers to as "villain's viewpoint" can reveal how the hero's best laid plans will be thwarted, thus heightening tension immeasurably. It's a device that can prove effective in almost any genre.

In general, if you're going to introduce more than one viewpoint, it's a good idea to put in a big enough chunk of each so your readers can adjust to it. My own tendency is to limit myself to not more than one viewpoint per chapter.

On the other hand, don't allow any viewpoint to run on so long that the others are forgotten.

Be sure to establish time, place, circumstance, and viewpoint each time you change, though. Not to do so is an open invitation to reader confusion—and irritation.

I'll talk about other viewpoint issues in the "long story" part of Chapter 14.

THE PROTAGONIST

The protagonist in a story is most often termed the hero or heroine. But that can be deceiving. Actually, the protagonist is the character who has a goal, the individual who's trying to achieve something.

A good case in point is *Crossing Delancey*, a play by Susan Sandler that later was made into a movie. At first glance it appeared to be a simple love story about a Jewish girl, clerk in a bookstore, who's moved Uptown from the Lower East Side. An East Side pickle peddler is her would-be suitor.

Who's the protagonist, girl or suitor?

Surprisingly enough, it's neither. The central figure, if you check closely, is the girl's Jewish grandmother, who's determined to see Girl married to a nice Jewish boy and secure in a traditional home.

Thing is, Girl is happy as she is. Boy isn't at all certain that Girl is the right bride for him. But Grandmother, unhappy because a change has come into her life — that is, Girl has abandoned her heritage for Uptown — has a goal: She's going to bring Girl back to her roots. To that end, she sets out to manipulate Girl into a proper marriage and acknowledgment of her Jewish values.

Do you see the pattern? As I've noted before, a story is the record of how somebody deals with danger. The protagonist is that somebody — a character made unhappy by a change in his or her situation and thus goal-motivated to a course of action that will return the happiness. Most often, that makes the protagonist what we commonly call the hero, but not always. Goal orientation or purpose is the issue.

Most often, too, the protagonist is the character readers care most about or are most interested in. But again, not always. The grandmother in *Crossing Delancey* has been so skillfully disguised that at first glance we tend to think of her as incidental, whereas actually she's the key to the puzzle.

What's your first step where building a protagonist is concerned, then? It's to ask yourself the essential question, "Whose story is this?" Because, believe me, it *is* somebody's, and that somebody is the person endangered, whether through threat to life, threat to happiness, or threat to dignity. Making the right decision as to who's threatened, choosing the right person for the role, is vital.

Note, too, that "protagonist" is a neutral term where sex is concerned. The old days when it automatically called forth masculine images is gone. Today, female protagonists often hold center stage.

It's also highly desirable to keep your protagonist an individual rather than a group. While we may cheer for a ball team, zeroing in on one player who has a private world to win or lose makes for an infinitely stronger effect.

So you have a proper hero or heroine. How do you make the story turn out "right," come to a proper conclusion?

You set your protagonist up with what I call climax potential. This means the protagonist has *two* things vitally important to him, not just one—love and security, for example; love being exemplified by a man or woman, security by the job he's always wanted, one tremendously desirable and with fantastic pay.

At the climax, your protagonist faces some form of physical or emotional disaster that forces him to choose between the two big things he cares about. The job, the security, offers an easy way out of an impending disaster. To choose the love side of the equation— the man or woman the protagonist yearns for—can lead only to cataclysm. (Or vice versa, of course. Love doesn't always triumph, nor does the other factor in the equation). But you plan and plant the story circumstances in such a manner that when Character makes the "right" choice—morally right, that is, in the view of your readers—he's rewarded with the happiness he sought at the story's beginning.

To cite Dashiell Hammett again, you'll find a beautiful example of this pattern in *The Maltese Falcon,* when at the climax Sam Spade gives up the woman he loves because his integrity is more important to him.

This also brings into focus the answer to another oft-asked question: Must a story always have a "happy" ending?

Answer: That depends on what Character sees as constituting happiness.

Thus, for Sam Spade, happiness meant being able to live with himself. So *The Maltese Falcon* had a happy—even though in its way tragic—ending.

Similarly, in a magazine novel I once wrote, the ending saw hero and heroine starting off up a mountain pursued by New Guinea headhunters. Odds were they'd end up dead meat at a cannibal barbeque. But for now they had each other, and if they died, they'd die together.

Readers loved it.

On the other hand, the other night I watched a play by a new playwright unfold. It was a skillful job, until the end. But the ending, unhappily, proved nothing, demonstrated nothing about the characters except that, in the old phrase, "Life is real, life is earnest, and we all die sometime." The audience left, muttering disappointment. Why? Because the story wasn't set up to provide the hero with an opportunity to make a meaningful choice, a decision that would leave the audience feeling fulfilled and satisfied. As it was, the hero had taken no stand that left him in a decisive position in relation to what the future might bring, so the story came to no real conclusion. It wasn't so planned as to give the protagonist climax potential.

Does a story have to have a happy ending? Not necessarily. After all, consider *Macbeth* or *Driving Miss Daisy,* which both end with the death of a main character. What you need is a *fitting* ending, one that is geared to the behavior of the character in the story. A good example is William Lindsay Gresham's *Nightmare Alley.* It concerns a carnival con man who exploits, corrupts, and robs virtually everyone with whom he comes in contact. The ending, which left *me* gasping, found him with only one road open—to become a "geek," a drunk who bites the heads off live chickens in a sideshow. Not a happy ending, certainly, but a *fitting* one the character had deserved.

Remember, too, that you, the writer, can make any ending happy if you build the characters in such a manner as to prove the protagonist worthy of happiness by his display, however subtly, of moral courage at the climax. Ever and always, the "right" ending is the satisfying ending, and a satisfying ending is happy.

Or, to put it another way, you the writer can make any ending a happy ending if you build your characters in such a manner as to give it meaning.

THE ANTAGONIST

The antagonist, in the popular view, is the villain.

Unfortunately, people tend to think of villains as wearing black hats and twirling the traditional long black mustache while they tie hapless, helpless Sophronia to the railroad tracks. The protagonist/hero is the noble soul on a white horse who comes to rescue her.

While you may find this pattern of good guy-versus-bad guy in many stories, it's far from a universally true picture these days. A villain may be better defined merely as Hero's opponent and so *antagonist.* Thus, he's not necessarily a bad person. He very well may be just as good a man as Hero. But if he gets what *he* wants, Hero can't achieve *his* heart's desire.

Consider, for example, two totally estimable astronauts, each seeking to be chosen for a Mars flight. Only one can go. That makes them antagonists. But you, the writer, by small details of phrasing and handling and choice of empathetic fragments of behavior, guide your audience to root for the one you've selected to win. That character is your hero.

Is the antagonist, the opponent, the villain, important? He is indeed. Dynamically speaking, he's probably more vital than your hero, for as old hands used to hammer at me when I was learning the trade, "The strength of your villain is the strength of your story."

You see, change, a disruption of your protagonist's *status quo,* is where your story starts. Protagonist just can't stand it, so he sets out to achieve a more satisfactory situation.

This brings him into conflict. Conflict with who? The antagonist, of course; the villain—for it's the villain who's instituted the change that's shattered your hero's *status quo.*

And as we've already pointed out with our astronauts, above, the villain quite possibly is just as decent a person as your hero. But he's determined to win, to have his own way. Therefore, he fights back ruthlessly against Hero—just as Hero would, were he in Villain's shoes.

Remember, then, that the villain is *not* necessarily villainous in the traditional sense. But he *is* determined and so he fights, meets Hero's efforts to restore Hero's *status quo* head-on.

Remember also that this isn't necessarily a battle that's waged with guns or daggers. It may involve no more than a developer's efforts to gain control of a sylvan valley for a subdivision, while an environmentalist hero seeks to preserve its beauty untouched for nature lovers. The key issue, for you, is that both sides are convinced they're right and both are willing to fight—with no bloodier weapons than votes or legal writs, quite possibly—to have their way.

THE LOVE INTEREST CHARACTER

Really, the only reason I feel it necessary to include the love interest character here is because, too often, he or she is pictured as merely a sexy part of the furniture.

Well, the sexy part is fine, especially if we substitute "desirable" for sexy. After all, beauty is in the eye of the beholder, as I've noted elsewhere. What counts is that Hero react favorably to the female paragon we set before him. Or, if the story is female-oriented, vice versa.

In these days, however, readers are no longer content to have the love component be just a mindless romance or sex romp. They insist that the female participant come through as a real person— that is, that she have goals and attitudes and preoccupations and a self-concept every bit as well-developed as her male compeer's. It makes for a more complex, more realistic, more interesting story. If you want an example, put a tape of *The African Queen* on your VCR and watch Katharine Hepburn in action.

THE BIT-PLAYERS

Often known as "incidental characters," these are the relatively minor actors in your fictional worlds. They're the passing suspects in mysteries, the incidental friends and co-workers and neighbors of Hero and Heroine, the waitresses and clerks and maintenance people who flesh out the cast.

You develop these to varying degrees, in accordance to their importance to your story. The more important ones should have some quirk, some bit of color or two that lift them above the dull gray level. Thus, a snuff-dipping man who repeatedly spits tobacco juice into a paper cup will be remembered, and so will a woman who wears black lipstick, or a child with a tendency to turn up in the wrong place at the wrong time in particularly irritating fashion. And that's fine.

Do bear in mind, though, that it's easy to become so intrigued with these bit-players that they come to dominate your story. A philosophical garbage man or a little old lady who fixes a beady eye through a cracked door on all visitors may mesh so perfectly with a clever line of dialogue that's popped into your head that you develop them further and so find them overshadowing your more important story people. For if you devote a lot of words to a character, that character automatically becomes important, simply because your readers assume that the fact that you gave him so much attention means *you* saw him as important to the tale you're telling.

What to do about it? The answer, of course, is to ask yourself, "Does this character advance the story with his cleverness or color

enough to warrant inclusion of all these lines or bits of business?"
If he doesn't, cut him back!

The same principle applies to your more important story people — Hero's or Heroine's intimates, Villain's henchmen, victims on
one level or another. Your story, ever and always, concerns one
primary figure: a protagonist whose happiness is threatened by a
change. All else is incidental and must be held to proper proportion.
And if you need an example, consider that great movie, *Casablanca,*
where the love story of Humphrey Bogart and Ingrid Bergman is
played out against a background of action and danger and a milling
host of colorful passing players. But the key word remains *passing,*
for those characters come and go and fall by the wayside, fascinating us while they hold the stage but never taking over to the point
that we lose sight of the heart of the story. Rick and his love for
Ilsa remain the core.

THE CHARACTER-IN-DEPTH

A high proportion of the time, story people tend to exist on one
level. Hero lives only to save Heroine from the clutches of a villain — the Batman syndrome, as it were. Hence, Hero is portrayed
only in terms of the brawn and brains necessary to fulfill that function, play that role.

People really aren't like that, of course. We each have a past, a
future, family, friends, job, reputation, beliefs, interests, prejudices,
and so on.

Too much of the time fictional characters are caricatures, creatures that rise little or not at all above first — that is, dominant —
impressions. Which is like our relationship with many people in
life. We never get above that level with them — after all, how inti-
mately do you know your postal carrier or taxi driver? When you
refer to a person as a "red-neck" or "yuppie" or "egghead," you're
setting him up as a caricature, a stereotype.

Building a character in depth means that you go beyond this.
Instead of limiting your picture of an offbeat high school boy to
such punk items as his purple mohawk haircut and the safety pin
through his left earlobe, you can introduce his unvoiced passion
for Jean Michel Jarre's New Age music and his tenderness towards
a crippled sister and his nightmares of his drunken father vomiting
on his dying mother and his secret fears that one day he'll kill
himself. You give him background, dreams, doubts, inner conflicts,

and the like, until the first impression/caricature with which you started becomes an excruciatingly detailed portrait. If you do it well, you may come up with a tremendously satisfying individual.

The danger is that if you go too far with this process you may create a being of such complexity and with so many facets that you lose your story. Goal orientation may submerge in soul searching, and life's trivia overwhelm dynamics. When that happens, a handful of intellectuals and academics may ponder and analyze your work, but it's unlikely to attract any mass readership.

I can give you no answer to this problem. You must decide for yourself to what degree you want realism to balance against situation-oriented tension, insight against excitement. For the issue *is* a matter of degree. Neither extreme is going to satisfy too many readers.

THE NON-HUMAN CHARACTER

Consider the amoeba as a character. The simplest of one-celled life forms, irregular and constantly changing in shape, it has direction in the sense that it's programmed to survive by projecting pseudopods to engulf its food. As an implacable, though non-malicious villain, it could do very well in a science fiction story, if only you could give it more meaningful emotion.

A number of writers have taken advantage of this kind of thinking to use animals as characters (Jack London with *Call of the Wild*), extraterrestrials (remember *E.T.*?), automata (Lester del Rey's classic "Helen O'Loy"), and so on.

The secret to writing about these creatures beyond the human pale really involves no skills beyond those you've already learned. In dealing with them, the key point to remember is that; precisely because humans can understand only humans, you must somehow endow your non-humans with human attributes, human traits.

Three questions will help you build such non-human beings both effectively and with minimum waste motion:

1. What are Alien's unique characteristics?
2. What does Alien have in common with your readers?
3. What is Alien's purpose?

Where Question 1 is concerned, it should be obvious enough

that Alien should somehow register as . . . well, alien; that is, non-human, as a ghost or a horse or a computer is non-human. And that is in no way a call for clichéd bug-eyed monsters, either. It may be enough that your other-worldly creature can read minds or walk through walls or reproduce via parthenogenesis or spontaneous generation or breaking off segments as do some kinds of starfish.

Question 2 zeroes in on the fact that it's essential for you to provide your alien with tags your audience can understand. Because that's how Godzilla, and the primitive in that delightful film, *The Gods Must Be Crazy,* and Hal the Computer from *2001,* and Black Beauty, and A. E. Van Vogt's Ptath successfully captured readers.

Or, as a science fiction artist once commented to me, "the simple way to make an alien monster acceptable to humans is to give it cocker spaniel eyes."

Which brings us to Question 3, and the fact that sad or warmly adoring cocker spaniel eyes simply aren't enough when you're building an alien in fiction. In addition, it's vital that you know Alien's purpose, what he/she/it is trying to do. He may not be able to voice it, you understand, so long as we lack a universe of discourse between species. But when snails invade your garden or cockroaches your kitchen, you have a pretty good idea of what they're after. Same for Greyfriars Bobby at his master's grave, and the billion little green men who invaded Earth in Fredric Brown's *Martians, Go Home!* On its own level and in its own way, each *feels,* and so, whether we love or hate them, we understand them.

Beyond which, projection, extrapolation, inference from established components—in a word, our old reliable *rationalization*— will provide you with the answer.

What's more to the point is to make sure you frame your non-human character in a story world that makes his goal-striving and emotion both human and logical. Thus, E.T. is understandable, makes sense to us, because he's stranded far from home. We know nothing about that home—nor do we need to. Homesickness is all we need. We understand it because we ourselves have felt it, so it gives us an emotional springboard from which to empathize with the little alien.

In the same way, the dog Buck in Jack London's *The Call of the Wild* reacts to the harshly brutal world into which the story plunges him in a manner that fits our own emotional patterns. We can understand his return to the savagery of his forebears on the basis of the stimuli to which he's subjected.

And so we end up back at the point from which we started: the importance, ever and always of emotion, feeling. It sparks well-nigh every story you read or write. Without it, your work is marked by happenstance and doomed to failure. With it, plus an understanding of basic story structure and character development, your chances for success are good.

So much for roles. But we've been serious about this writing business long enough. It's time we took a break, looked at the lighter side of things, humor, and how you can create it and adapt it to your story.

We'll explore it in the next chapter.

11

THE LIGHT TOUCH

How do you make a character amusing?
You replace reader assumptions
with offbeat alternatives.

How do you give a character or story a light touch? What's the secret of "amusing"? Those are questions on which most of us have pondered at one time or another.

People do like to laugh, though. Ask Bob Hope, Phyllis Diller, Bill Cosby, Art Buchwald, Daniel Pinkwater, Garrison Keillor, Anne Tyler, Roseanne Barr, or your friendly neighborhood TV gagman if you don't believe me.

Where you as a writer are concerned, humor and its low-key cousin, the amusing, often are next to vital, and not just on account of their reader appeal. In addition, they're useful tools for changing pace, reducing tension, adding proportion, neutralizing purple prose, and maybe even unscrewing the inscrutable.

Further, there's a simple approach, once you understand the issues. But said understanding *is* important. Without it, you can grope and fumble endlessly.

The thing to remember is that the amusing character actually is a character whose roots lie in humor.

So, what *is* humor? How do you handle it?

Answer: Humor is first and foremost a state of mind, and said state varies drastically from individual to individual. Attitude is the issue—an attitude or character trait we call a sense of humor.

Before a character can have a sense of humor, *you* must. Do you view the world through slightly skewed, laugh-tinted glasses? Do you see people and events with which you come in contact as funny? Is it your habit to chuckle—perhaps involuntarily—at things others take at face value?

Fine! The fact that you react thus constitutes a good start when it comes to creating lighthearted story moods and ludicrous or pleasantly entertaining people and situations. Beyond that, once you learn humor's underlying principles, applying them to your story people will soon be second nature.

So, forward, and forgive me if I seem to take the long way around, through cartoons and jokes and gag definitions and mirth-provoking verse en route to where we discuss the actual creation of humorous and amusing characters and situations. It's necessary, believe me, if you're to understand the issues.

WHAT HAPPENS IN HUMOR?

Laughter is the noise a person makes when he or she attains release from the tyranny of the "should."

Humor is a device designed to do this releasing. It's a trigger, a detonating cap, a mental tickle.

To make people laugh, you devise a plausible (and quite possibly ridiculous), yet unanticipated alternative for something that *is* or *is supposed to be* a certain way. Then, you call attention to this alternative in such a manner that the reader or auditor abruptly becomes aware of both its contrast with and its similarity to the norm.

In other words, implicitly or explicitly your reader anticipates one thing, then unexpectedly gets another. Yet what he gets makes sense, in its own warped way, and no damage is done, and so he laughs.

Exhibit A: A cartoon shows three ghosts in a spooky-looking attic. Two, garbed in white sheets, are talking. The third, silent and the obvious object of the discussion, wears a black sheet. Punchline: "This is Cousin Adolph, the black sheep of the family."

Where's the humor in it?

To find out, we need to consider four points:

1. The *assumption* which exists in the reader's mind . . . the *should,* the expectation, the "This-is-the-way-things-like-this-are-supposed-to-be."
2. The *alternative* to this assumption which the humorist offers . . . the unanticipated deviation from established pattern.

3. The *applicability* of the humorist's use of the alternative . . . the element of warped plausibility which forces the reader to concede, "Yes, it *might* happen this way, if you grant the right premise."

4. The *abruptness* with which the reader becomes aware of the alternative's contrast to the assumed norm, the situation.

Now, applying this pattern of analysis to our ghost cartoon, what do we find?

1. *Assumption:* The world follows certain rules, even where ghosts are concerned. Specifically, ghosts *should*—are supposed to—wear white sheets.

2. *Alternative:* Here is a ghost who deviates from the established pattern. He wears a *black* sheet.

3. *Applicability:* The alternative is made rational, plausible, in a warped fashion by the play-on-words and play-on-ideas of the punchline.

   a.) "Black sheet" is an obvious pun—a twisting of language that provides an applicable yet unanticipated alternative for the assumption that the words *should* add up to the familiar phrase, "black sheep."

   b.) Most of us also assume that ghosts are ghosts. That is, we take it for granted that (1.) ghosts are uniquely different from humans, and (2.) all ghosts are the same. Our cartoon, however, confronts us with a plausible yet unanticipated alternative for this idea, this stereotype: Ghosts, it in effect says, react like people; and, like people, they sit in judgment on each other.

4. *Abruptness:* Attention is called to the alternative approach suddenly and unexpectedly, with a punchline that brings out the point of the gag in a five-word phrase at the *end* of the sentence.

Exhibit B: Here we have a joke:

"Doctor, I'm worried," says the patient to his psychiatrist. "I'm always talking to myself."

"Is that really so bad?" the psychiatrist probes. "Lots of people do that."

"Yes, Doctor, I know," responds the patient. "But I'm such a bore."

1. *Assumption:* That the *act* of talking is what's bothering the patient.
2. *Alternative:* The *content* of the talking actually is the issue.
3. *Applicability:* Much as we may hate to admit it, all of us have been bored with ourselves, at one time or another. So the patient's statement *does* make sense, even though it's so far out as to reduce logic to absurdity.
4. *Abruptness:* The *very last word* in the story is the stinger!

Exhibit C: A gag definition:

"Sympathy is what one girl gives another in exchange for details."

1. *Assumption:* Kindness and concern are supposed to be the key motives for sympathy.
2. *Alternative:* In actuality, avidity for scandal and a desire to gloat over the other fellow's troubles frequently serve as our point of focus.
3. *Applicability:* The truth of the alternative, and the wry, cold-turkey frankness with which it is set against the politely platitudinous stereotype, are obvious.
4. *Abruptness:* Again, the arrangement of the line is such that the punch comes at the very end. And the word "details" captures the exact nuances of both connotation and denotation beautifully.

Exhibit D: Let's look at a familiar fragment of humorous verse:

> See the happy moron;
> He doesn't give a damn.
> I wish I were a moron—
> My God! Perhaps I am!

1. *Assumption:* Mental deficiency is something that afflicts somebody else.

2. *Alternative:* It just might be that we're not as sharp as we think we are.
3. *Applicability:* Haven't we all some time or other given lip service to how fortunate the stupid are, in their alleged freedom from responsibility and worry?
4. *Abruptness:* Rhyme and timing put the punch where it belongs—cleverly phrased, at the end of the verse.

Now few writers deal with such rigidly structured forms as those set forth above. But we all may very well make use of the same principles in giving our copy an occasional light touch.

For example, consider this line from Lilian Jackson Braun's *The Cat Who Knew Shakespeare:*

> *"Mr. President," said Susan Exbridge, "I would like to make a proposal. The Singing Society will present Handel's Mes-siah at the Old Stone Church on November twenty-fourth, exactly as it was performed in period costume. We had planned a reception for the performers afterward, and this museum would be a marvelous place to have it, if Mr. Qwil-leran would consent."*
>
> *"Okay with me," said Qwilleran, "provided I don't have to wear satin knee breeches."*

1. *Assumption:* A straight statement/question will get a straight answer.
2. *Alternative:* The person responding may take the state-ment/question lightly—as when Qwilleran tacks on the facetious bit, "provided I don't have to wear satin knee breeches."
3. *Applicability:* The satin knee breeches line is perfect counterpoint to Susan Exbridge's statement "exactly as it was performed in period costume."
4. *Abruptness:* The stinger phrase appears *at the end* of the sentence, where it will jolt the reader most.

Here's another case in point, from Sharyn McCrumb's *Paying the Piper.* Describing her boyfriend, the viewpoint character says:

> *". . . Cameron's heart is* not *in the Highlands; it is probably*

not attached to his brain; it may even be in a jar of formalde-
hyde in an Edinburgh University biology lab."

The Robert Burns line about "My heart's in the Highlands" is used as a jumping-off point for reversal, exaggeration, incongruity, and unanticipated manipulation of words. Yet the result is plausible enough, applicable enough, when viewed in the right light — which is to say, the proper mood of openness to fun via drollery.

Finally, scan these lines from Marissa Piesman's *Unorthodox Practices:*

Nina stared at the heading on the Chinese menu. Pork. Chicken. Beef. Seafood. Noodles. Each gave her a little thrill. Nina felt a certain way in Chinese restaurants. A way she felt nowhere else. The way an old-time alkie must feel in a broken-down gin mill. A sense of familiarity and comfort tinged with guilt. Only around Chinese food did Nina drop even a semblance of vigilance and eat like a pig. Like Aunt Sophie at the Viennese table at a bar mitzvah. Like Albert Finney in Tom Jones. *Like the girls in the dorm on a heavy marijuana night. There had been a lot of magazine talk lately about comfort food. Cookbooks written on mashed potatoes, chicken pot pie, and macaroni and cheese. Shrimp with lobster sauce was Nina's comfort food. It certainly tasted better than anything her mother had ever actually cooked.*

The unanticipated, yet applicable, alternative to the *should* abounds here. The stereotyped norm is under fire from all directions. Thus, people are supposed to *order* from a menu, Chinese or otherwise, not *thrill* to the items listed. Her state of mind is compared to that of an alcoholic in a decaying bar, so that she develops a "sense of familiarity and comfort tinged with guilt." Fastidiousness is replaced by such gross gluttony that she eats "like a pig," or even her Aunt Sophie or Albert Finney. The whole passage is a paroxysm of exaggeration, warped analogy, and compulsive food fetishism, and the picture it paints gives Nina a dimension of which we were previously unaware, even while it provides amusement.

How does all this add up to laughter? Let's take another look at our original hypothesis:

Laughter is the noise a person makes when he or she attains release from the tyranny of the "should."

What is this *should* I talk about? How is it a tyrant?

Life gives us our answer: The world is *supposed* to be a certain way. People and things *should* act as expected, stay consistent to their established specifications and characteristics and behavior patterns, with fire forever hot, ice cold, guns lethal, and kittens playful.

Now you and I know, however, that *should* and *is* very well may prove to be miles apart, and we have the Kinsey and Hite reports to prove it. But from Socrates and Galileo on down it's been treason to suggest such. In the view of most people, most of the time, anything that contradicts the way things are assumed and anticipated to be is potentially dangerous. Those who deviate from the foreordained idea constitute menaces to society. And this is the case whether the issue be physical, intellectual, or moral.

In a word, the *should* becomes a tyrant to enslave us, rule our lives. We're brought up in the belief that we *should* behave according to set standards and convictions of our culture because, implicitly, not to do so may prove disastrous. What started out as rough rule of thumb, a crude map scratched in sand to guide us, now burgeons forth as ironclad law.

Entering any situation, therefore, you're to a degree alert, which is to say tense — muscles at least a fraction contracted in preparation for potential fight or flight in case danger looms. Awareness of new experience always creates this tension. If you perceive no hazard, no departure from the way you feel the situation *should* be, your tension eases.

But now suppose that what you discover, far from fitting into the preconceived scheme of things dictated by the *should,* is an extreme and unanticipated deviation from what you expected.

If the discovery comes abruptly enough, and if elements of similarity between anticipated and unanticipated may be observed clearly enough, and if the new state of affairs, though startling, plunges you into no real danger and does you no real damage, and if you're in the right mood, then your tension may be released suddenly in that succession of rhythmic, spasmodic expirations with open glottis and vibration of the vocal folds that we call laughter.

That is, you've met the unanticipated, the deviation from the *should*, and it hasn't proved disastrous. The shock of discovering it ridiculous instead of dangerous has triggered release of your pent-up tension in a muscular paroxysm, pleasurable instead of painful. You've attained release from the tyranny of the should.

In other words, you laughed.

Or at least smiled.

And if you didn't—?

Odds are that it's for one or more of seven reasons . . . seven key points at which anyone's attempt at humor may go astray:

1. You didn't start with a clearly defined *should* . . . a way things are supposed to be.

Humor begins with assumption, anticipation. Further, this assumption must be one held by or at least familiar to your readers. If you have no mental image of a standard, how can you be aware of—let alone appreciate—deviations from that standard? For a sweet little old lady's inappropriate behavior to be funny to you, you must first have a picture in your head of just how sweet little old ladies *do* or *should* act. We must have expectations where they're concerned. Same for cops, robbers, lovers, mothers-in-law, shipwrecked sailors, and all the other traditional comic figures.

Including unique, individual story people of your own creation!

The same principle applies to situations, places, things. Funerals are supposed to be solemn, hospitals quiet, cars mobile, and so on.

Here, however, we need to bear another key fact in mind: People laugh at *reaction* rather than action—and situations and places and things don't react.

Consider, for example, the man who turns on a faucet. Instead of the normal flow expected, a great gush of water spouts forth, drenching him. When onlookers laugh, it's at the man's actual or imagined startlement/outrage at the unanticipated turn of events, rather than the event itself. The faucet is only a means to an end. The victim's reaction is the issue.

Same way, a major reason people like anecdotes is because they're interested in seeing how the central character *reacts* to danger or adversity or embarrassment or the unanticipated.

Often, of course, especially in jokes, the reaction is implicit. The reader or auditor visualizes what the central character is anticipating—and the shock with which he'll respond to the unanticipated. You don't have to actually *see* someone's pants fall down in order to know that it will discomfit the person to whom it happens.

Humor of character frequently is based on emotional reactions inappropriate or incongruous to a given situation. The unique personal approach the character takes is manifested in overreaction, underreaction, or unanticipated reaction. Thus, naive calm in the presence of a man-eating Bengal tiger . . . extreme upset over a burnt piece of toast . . . responding to the butterfly perched on a nude girl's knee rather than to the girl's nudity . . . all these are productive of humor, and all are based on the idea that there is a set and accepted way of reacting to such dilemmas and situations.

The *should* in language is equally obvious. Its roots lie in our assumption that there is a standard of grammar, of structure, of definition, and that proper people will bow to the rules. Then, along comes dialect, warping all the regulations in the name of the foreigner's unfamiliarity with English, and we collapse in gales of hilarity. Or a pun harmlessly punctures our pretensions of knowledge, our mental image of the applicability of a given word, and we laugh at how neatly it fits into the unanticipated context.

A factor which also enters here and in much other humor is inflation of ego — the feeling of superiority that comes when actual or potential ridicule focuses on a character. We know how something's supposed to be said. When Character reveals his ignorance, we automatically glory in the fact that we know better.

Process, especially, offers unlimited possibilities for this kind of ego-boo, with a whole series of *shoulds* linked together. This is why so much slapstick comedy centers on someone trying to hang a screen or paper a wall or bake a pie. One funny twist acts as springboard to another; mirth mounts; repetition of a bit (the so-called "running gag") intensifies the effect, and the audience rolls in the aisles.

And so it goes. The thing to remember is that one way or another, implicitly or explicitly, humor always is predicated on a *should*. That's why it's so often claimed that there are only a dozen or so basic jokes. It's not that just drunks or taxes or politicians or stinginess are funny; it's that *our attitudes* are clearly set where such subjects are concerned. They're the areas with the broadest, most familiar *shoulds*. The rules in relation to Ornithischia or nuclear theory or theosophy may be every bit as rigid, but not as many people know about them. So, the chances of a general reader reacting to humor built around them are likely to be slim.

Does this mean you must abandon such subjects?

On the contrary. It merely demands that you build up a picture to knock down . . . create an image of a *should.*

After which, it might be to your advantage to take an even harder look at the alternatives that it implies.

2. The alternative isn't far enough removed from the *should.*

There's a thing called subtlety. In humor it can very easily be carried too far.

Contrast is the issue.

What is contrast? It's the exhibition of noticeable differences between things when they're compared or set side by side.

For most of us, it's difficult to distinguish instantly between a 1988 Ford and a 1989 Ford. The contrast between them isn't marked enough, in our eyes. Same way for perfumes, mentholated cigarettes, women's hats, and old crime movies on TV.

If you're reasonably literate, you'll be amused by such student boners as "An epistle is the wife of an apostle," or "An unbridled orgy is a wild horse," or "Ambiguity means having two wives living at the same time." But there also are segments of the population that will greet such sallies with blank stares.

The conclusion for you to draw from this is that if the issue is humor and you're in search of a wide audience, you'd better select an alternative markedly different from the chosen *should.* So different, in fact—in content or presentation or intention—that it *can't* be taken seriously.

Sometimes direct reversal is the answer here—the Texan who buys his dog a boy, the village where nothing happens every minute, the cannibal who walks into a restaurant and orders a waiter. But more often if suffices—especially in non-joke humor—merely to examine common assumptions about your subject, then deviate as far as your imagination will allow.

Thus, scientists are supposed to be brilliant. Deviate slightly, and we get an inept scientist—and because he's merely inept, he's likely to prove more painful or piteous than funny. Difference from the accepted *should* is insufficient. It must be different to a degree that reduces the *should* to absurdity.

Suppose, then, that instead of just making our scientist inept, we picture him as impossibly stupid—a bumbling little man, a laboratory janitor, with incongruous pretensions to being a scientist. At once, he takes on comic overtones and everything he does holds the potentiality of humor.

In the same way, a person with a vestigial tail is victim of a minor physical handicap, to be remedied by surgery as soon as possible. Give the entire human race long, bushy tails and you have an unanticipated alternative to the *should* of accepted human development that H. Allen Smith built to book length in that wild volume entitled *The Age of the Tail.*

How many young women have dated sailors? Ruth McKenney multiplied the situation by five Brazilian naval cadets in a classic of yesteryear, *My Sister Eileen.* It made her a fortune.

All of us daydream of transcending physical law. Marcel Ayme translated that fantasy into *The Man Who Walked Through Walls.* Care to try to imagine an alternative farther from its *should* than that?

3. The alternative to the *should* lacks applicability.

To have humorous applicability, an alternative must epitomize the contradiction between *should* and unanticipated deviation.

Applicability means that a sort of implicit analogy exists between assumption and alternative; a clearly recognizable parallel between what we expect and what we get. The two situations, though not the same, have certain key points in common.

If such a parallel doesn't exist, we have difference, but not necessarily humor.

Take, for example, a cartoon in which a stenographer enters a room where a man lies immersed in a bath. The man says, "Excuse me for not rising, Miss Glutz."

The humor in this, such as it is, centers on the fact that for the man to rise would violate our society's nudity taboo—a strong, sexually oriented *should.* When he says, "Excuse me for not rising," he calls attention to this issue with a familiar phrase entirely acceptable to closely analogous situations. And this, of course, pinpoints the contradiction, the contrast between alternative and *should.*

Suppose, instead, that the punchline had been delivered by the stenographer: "Shall I take those letters now, Mr. Glutz?"

Unanticipated deviation from the norm? To a degree.

Funny? Not very.

Why? Because the *should* that surrounds conditions under which stenographers may take dictation is much less rigid than the one governing nudity. Hence, there's less contradiction to epitomize; hence, less applicability of alternative to *should;* hence, less humor.

In other words, applicability, like almost everything else in this world, is a matter of degree, with some alternatives riotous, others tired or dreary, others complete washouts.

Now let's try another switch. This time, we'll leave the punchline the same, "Excuse me for not rising, Miss Glutz." But we'll replace the stenographer with a sexy-looking blonde in a negligee.

Applicability: nil. Humor: nil.

Why? Because we no longer have an applicable alternative. Girl in negligee plus man in bathtub equals a sex-oriented situation. So even though the man's line is unanticipated, it comes out banal instead of funny, because it expresses no real contradiction, no true conflict between *should* and *is*. It does *not* call attention to the point of the gag, because no point exists.

In contrast, consider Charles Addams's famous panel that shows ski-tracks on a snowy landscape. There's a tree in the foreground. The tracks indicate that one ski went on one side of the tree, the other on the other.

Here our assumption, our *should,* says that trees are something you go around when you're on skis. With *both* skis on *one* side.

Unanticipated alternative: In this particular case, one ski goes on one side, the other on the other, in direct violation of physical possibility.

Which *can't* be — but here it is — only how — ?

Contradiction epitomized. Reality contravened. An alternative so applicable yet unexplainable that the cartoon sticks in your memory for years.

In summary, then . . . the unanticipated alternative must hold strong elements of the familiar . . . must have clear-cut points in common with the *should,* so that it may capture and pinpoint the ridiculousness of the situation, the absurdity of the contrast between what's shown or described and what's supposed to be.

Naturally, alternatives that fill such a bill of particulars are ever so easy to find. Ask any humor writer along about 2:00 A.M. some morning, when he finally gives up hunting for the apt phrase and deft twist and heads for the nearest bottle because he's too frustrated to go to bed.

But at least now you know just what it is you're hunting!

4. The differences that distinguish alternative from assumption aren't sufficiently emphasized.

Earlier, we said that contrast lies close to the heart of humor. It's rooted in the disparity between assumption and alternative, *should* and *is*. But it's one thing for a disparity to exist; another for your reader to recognize and laugh about it.

Your two most useful tools for bringing this disparity into focus, and thus sharpening your humor, are *exaggeration* and *incongruity*. The one throws a spotlight on the point at issue. The other places that point in a situation where its difference from the norm stands out.

Exaggeration means overstatement, understatement, distortion. You may exaggerate situation, character, reaction, language — you name it. Exaggeration of anything, carried to an extreme, equals reduction to absurdity.

You overstate when you refer to a woman after a Cub Scout den meeting as a "broken figure." Or when, as an example of her husband's penuriousness, you say that he expects their children to make all-day suckers last a week. You understate when you claim a girl's figure makes a fencepost's look good, or that you need a job so bad you're willing to pay the boss to let you work. You distort when you give a man's Adam's apple inordinate attention, or emphasize a dowager's pouter-pigeon bosom to a ludicrous degree, or otherwise overstate or understate part of a whole.

Incongruity, in turn, strikes a jarring note between elements with which you work. It's the beautiful girl with the 96-pound weakling as a favored suitor; the prospector boiling the beans who offers his partner a menu; the rabbit riding in a kangaroo's pouch. The inappropriate, the inconsistent, the contradictory, the paradoxical, the reverse English twist — all are incongruous and, hence, help to intensify our awareness of contrast, deviation from the norm, and humor.

5. Awareness of the contrast doesn't come abruptly.
A joke is like a scorpion. The stinger belongs in the tail.
Similarly, in non-joke humor, timing is crucial.

What do we mean by timing? We mean that you present a key fragment of material at the moment when it will achieve maximum humorous effect.

When is that moment? It's when the shock of contrast between assumption and alternative is most marked, most clearly defined.

In other words, the thing you need to strive for is to throw the elements with which you're working into juxtaposition in such a way and at such a time as will enable your reader to see for himself, instantly, that the result is funny, as illustrated in examples earlier in this chapter. Failure to do so will put you in the position of the speaker who forgets the point of a joke.

6. The subject is too serious, too disturbing emotionally to your reader or audience.

"The most valuable sense of humor," someone once observed, "is the kind that enables a person to see instantly what it isn't safe to laugh at."

When we say that a story is the record of how somebody deals with danger, we must remember that dangers fall into three major categories. The first, basis for much of melodrama, may be termed the threat to life. The second category, foundation stone of less sensational drama, is the threat to happiness. Finally, we have the threat to vanity, from which springs most comedy, most humor.

Vanity is based on ego, conceit. Our basic vanity lies in the implicit assumption we all make that the world is the way we see it, and that others view us as we ourselves do, and that what we anticipate will always come to pass; that reality will conform to our picture of it.

Humor punctures vanity, by revealing that we may not always be right in these assumptions. We laugh when, abruptly and in an unanticipated manner, it comes to our attention that it's possible to find applicable yet ridiculous alternatives to our picture of reality.

But the moment an event moves out of the category of threat to vanity, and over into that of threat to happiness or threat to life, humor ends. A fat man slipping on a banana peel is funny — until, in the fall, he breaks his back. Drunks are amusing, but not alcoholics. Race, marital infidelity, war, crime — our view of each changes any time it's brought into focus as a real problem.

Especially is this true when we find ourselves in the center of things. There are no good losers, only good actors, as the saying goes. Or, to quote the late Will Rogers, "Everything is funny as long as it is happening to somebody else."

So, we appreciate the puncturing of vanity best when it's the other fellow's ego that takes the beating. Step into a mudhole that fills your shoes with slime and water, and most of us register irritation. Watch someone else do the same thing, and we double over with laughter.

The man whose insecurities force him to build his feelings of self-worth on vanity rather than achievement may prove completely devoid of a sense of humor; or, he may do all his laughing at others . . . fly into a rage when anyone laughs at him.

Is it possible to make even the serious funny? To a degree, yes.

a.) Avoid the viewpoint of people too emotionally involved in the subject's tragic aspects.

A mother whose child has just been killed by a hit-and-run driver is hardly in a position to deal with the event lightly.

b.) Limit and de-emotionalize attention devoted to the unpleasant side of things.

A flood may be a disaster. But it's always possible to ignore the floating corpses or the heart-broken old couple whose life savings have been swept away, in favor of a man and three cats stranded high in a tree.

c.) Focus on the ridiculous side—especially the behavior of the people involved.

Observe the discovery of a body, a la Sharyn McCrumb in *Bimbos of the Death Sun:*

> *Louis Warren tried the door handle. It wasn't locked, so he eased his way into the room, wondering whether Dungannon was present, and about to hurl a lamp at his head, or absent, or planning to have him arrested for breaking and entering. Perhaps he ought to leave a note.*
>
> *The only sound in the room was the clack of the printer. Warren looked at the unmade bed, the row of bottles on the window ledge, the cowboy hat atop the computer monitor, and finally at Appin Dungannon, seated in a chair by the desk.*
>
> *He looked much as usual: bulging piggy eyes, gargoyle face, unfashionably long hair. . . . The pallor was a change from his usual boozy redness, though, and the stain on his*

shirt was definitely not Chivas Regal. . . . Louis Warren kept staring at the body, idly wondering if he had two more wishes coming.

Finally the shock wore off of it, and he stumbled back into the hall, nearly colliding with a tall, dark-cloaked vampire. "Excuse me," murmured Louis Warren. "I wonder if you would know anything about death?"

And so it goes. Murder isn't funny. But, upon occasion, writers like Craig Rice and Frank Gruber and Fredric Brown have certainly made it seem so!

7. **The final key to why humor may go astray is that a playful mood hasn't been established at the beginning, which leaves the reader unprepared to laugh.**

Listen to how Gillian Roberts begins *Caught Dead in Philadelphia:*

At 7:58 A.M. on a wet Monday morning, twenty-seven hours after giving up cigarettes and a green-eyed disc jockey, I was not in a mood to socialize. Facing myself in the bathroom mirror had exhausted my conviviality. Choosing a sweater and skirt had used up my intellectual reserve.

Here's Robert Barnard starting off *The Cherry Blossom Corpse:*

"Oh look, darlings, cherry blossom," said Amanda Fairchild, as we sped from the docks into the center of Bergen, and towards the bus station. She added, with a cat-like smile: "Especially for me."

I didn't tell her it was apple, and I didn't ask why it should be thought to be especially for her. I'd already had Amanda Fairchild up to here.

Or consider the first line of Jim Stinson's *Truck Shot:*

Filmmaking is always nine parts boredom, but staring for hours at a pregnant goldfish was threatening to push tedium across the threshold of pain.

The issue here, of course, is that if you propose to write humor, for heaven's sake put your reader in a mood for it *from the start.* Unless you do, he may never get around to laughing at all.

In point of fact, without the right mood, humor is as likely to irritate as entertain. Remember your feelings of frustration when that banquet speaker suddenly, in mid-address, brought in an allusion which could have been intended as funny—but could, equally well, have represented pure ineptitude? You have to be in a playful frame of mind to enjoy being tickled; and humor is a mental tickle!

The solution, obviously, is to follow the trail broken by past experts. From your first line, show by selection and exaggeration, incongruity and irony, metaphor and situation, that you intend to amuse as well as excite. You can begin, "The hair Elsa twisted about her finger had all the sheen and life of a tangle of wet fishline." Or you can start out, "Elsa's hair hung limp and lustreless." But the smile for which the first prepares your reader can very well pay off in heartier laughter later on . . . and the lack of that same smile in the second may prove the reason why your best efforts at achieving a light twist failed to touch the reader at the climax.

HOW TO COAX SMILES

It's one thing to analyze the other fellow's humor, another to coax smiles from readers with your own.

How best to start? Cultivate a sense of the ridiculous. Hunt for chances to laugh. Open your eyes to incongruity and contradiction. Twist. Distort. Exaggerate. Draw absurd parallels.

Then, write.

Any don'ts?

1. Don't try to get by with a weak story.

Would-be humorists tend to think that laughter alone will carry the ball. They're wrong. Start, always, with a yarn strong enough to stand alone if written with no attempt at the amusing.

2. Don't fail to establish your humor as humor.

If you're writing a funny story, let your reader know it by using humorous metaphors and phrasings from the beginning—and that means right from the very first line.

As part of this, it won't hurt a bit if you give the humorous character amusing traits in keeping with his personality, dynamics, and background. Is he the kind of person who'd get out of the pool into which he'd fallen with a remark about "those goldfish being too darned fast," or at a dinner party would he observe that his host or hostess must be subsidized by a diet clinic?

The thing to remember, always, is that attitude (yours and Character's) and content determine whether a line is straight or light. Whatever goes on, it's important that you focus on the way Character sees things and what he says or thinks about them, whether he views what's happening as dead serious or amusing.

Thus, Hero discovers that his ex-con contact, conditioned by years in prison, keeps cockroaches as pets. His comment: "Lively little devils, aren't they? Though I really prefer the big ones you get down in Panama."

Contrast this with a "straight" handling: "Edwards' stomach turned. The insects' movements had the slowly roiling quality of water just beginning to boil. 'You mean, you can eat with these things on the same table?' he choked."

Or again: "Linda asked, 'Don't you ever get lonely?' 'Not unless I'm with people,' Carl answered wryly," as contrasted with "Carl looked away. He didn't answer."

In other words, if it's amusing, present it in amusing terms. Like everything else in humor, this means to work with the assumption/ alternative pattern, in terms of both a character's thinking and speech. In each of the cited examples, you tend to expect one thing, but you get another.

(What if your handling is third-person objective, not entering Character's mind? Then you describe what goes on in objective terms, of course, setting forth what happens as if you were a camera that focuses on details that you feel likely to prove amusing to your readers.)

If a scene or incident in a serious story is supposed to be humorous, set the tone at once, the same way you'd prepare your readers for a change in time or place or circumstance or viewpoint.

If the issue is a comic relief character, paint her in amusing terms from the moment of her introduction. And it won't hurt a bit if, in that introduction, she is caught up in an amusing situation or behaves in an amusing manner.

Finally,

3. Don't play gag-writer.

Gags tend to dominate a story. They're great for stand-up comics, but there's little place for them in fiction.

Humor is, instead, a tone, a mood. It should be indigenous to a story or scene or character — not something extraneous, stuck on after the fact like a corn-plaster.

And beyond this?

You can plough through Bergson, Eastman, and Freud, of course . . . master long lists of sure-fire humor formulae and topics . . . argue at length as to whether drive to superiority ranks higher than embarrassment as a source of mirth.

But in all honesty, intellectualization is not the answer. No approach, no system, no formulation can claim to stand as definitive; and that includes the things I've said here. Ever and always, humor is subjective. The secret in coaxing smiles lies less in study and methodology than it does in avoiding them. Once you understand the basic laugh mechanism, the principle of the unanticipated alternative, be content to let your subconscious do the work. Believe me, it may surprise you.

Stay aware, always, that a story is the record of how somebody deals with danger. In humor, the danger is primarily a threat to vanity, an assault on man's conviction that he knows all the answers.

Your problems, if any, will tend to revolve around your search for apt alternatives — unanticipated deviations from the norm that you can shape into smiles.

Your starting point in attacking this problem quite possibly will be a list of the assumptions your readers normally would make about your subject — the *shoulds* from which you propose to deviate, whether your topic be horseflies or society matrons or bowling alleys or ways to describe a ball-point pen.

There follows focused free association. If your subject is a person, then you know that he or she may be considered in terms of appearance, speech, behavior, and habit of thought, multiplied by past and future and then extended a dozen steps beyond infinity via similarity, contrast, and contiguity. Exaggeration enters, and so does incongruity. Soon you find yourself with a retired speech professor who stutters or a millionaire given to haggling over a penny sales tax.

And if your hero glances apprehensively at the huge armchair to which he's been directed, because "It had a hungry look about it," some unwary reader just may break down enough to smile.

All this is extraneous to another issue, however — one that calls for immediate attention. It's the vital importance of the words with which you portray your characters as they move through your story.

We'll take it up in the next chapter.

12

THE RIGHT WORDS

*How do you describe a
character effectively?
You build the character with
significant specifics that lead readers to
feel the way you want them to feel.*

The thing I remember about the old woman is the big, hairy mole that grew on her right cheek midway between nose and chin. Her name, her face, her body—those are details long forgotten. I have a vague residual impression that she was one of my mother's friends; that's all. But I still remember the mole.

Then there was Gwen, younger sister of one of my boyhood buddies. She was pale and blonde and slender, I recall. But what really struck you about her was the fact that her lips were a vivid blue, consequence of some sort of heart ailment that, in those days, was beyond treatment.

Or consider Sam, who stuttered, or Mack, who drank, or Enos, the little banty rooster of a man who fought and refought the World War II battle for Leyte till friends would walk around the block to avoid another repetition of the story.

Why do I open this chapter on words and character description with such recollections? For one simple reason: Your goal, when you write a story, is to create or evoke *feeling* in your reader, because he reads in order to experience feeling. If you don't touch him on the feeling level, sooner or later—sooner, in all likelihood—he'll stop reading.

Further, feelings about virtually everything already exist within your reader. Your task is merely to devise ways to bring them forth. Therefore, most often, you write about characters, because as people ourselves we're naturally curious and interested in the human animal and how it functions. Reading about them, your reader shares the feelings one or more of them feel. If you could achieve the same results with algebraic formulae, we'd all be mathematicians.

The principle involved here is simple enough. You want your reader to draw his own conclusions as to what's going on, how the characters feel. You do this by giving him appropriate stimuli to react to . . . in terms of sensory perceptions, not prepackaged emotions which he may or may not accept. You don't just tell him "This person is nice." The trick is to show Character doing nice things. Whereupon, Reader will form an opinion of his own, rather than having to rely upon another person's judgment.

Why? Because we always trust our own experience more than what someone else tells us.

Your most effective stimuli for getting through to readers thus are what are termed "significant details": details that both individualize the character and evoke the desired feelings about him.

A character notices things according to what's important to him at the moment. If you're an alcoholic desperate for a drink, the clink of glassware may loom large for you. As a burglar on a midnight foray, you quite possibly magnify every sound that hints at a door opening. Light is the enemy in a photographer's darkroom.

You, as author, must decide what's significant. What feelings, what effect, do you want? It's only common sense to select material that you think will evoke it . . . arrange it in an effective order . . . describe it to fit Character's personality and tension level. The external stimuli and sensory details which will best bring the chosen feelings forth are the significant ones.

To this end, often, the key issue is what to leave out.

Which is?

Deadwood. Generalities. Empty words—words that apply to anyone, words that tell the reader nothing meaningful and so don't develop the characters or advance the plot by changing the situation in terms of someone's state of affairs or state of mind. Details about the character that confuse the reader, as when a smart person does a dumb thing. Or a description of Character's ingrown toenail when it has no bearing on the action.

More specifically, you need to pick out and zero in on the salient/significant/symbolic features that distinguish Character as an individual and make him or her memorable, while at the same time evoking feelings in him and in the reader. All else is secondary and to be subordinated.

In brief, you select, arrange, and describe your material in such a way as to achieve a predetermined effect.

Take Stevenson's Long John Silver as a case in point. What image flashes into your mind's eye when you think of him? And any of you who fail to answer, "His peg leg, of course," may consider yourselves slapped on the wrist in spirit. By introducing a significant detail, Stevenson has both individualized him and raised intriguing questions that evoke curiosity — a feeling to keep readers reading.

Similarly, Sherlock Holmes bears labels and tags recognized in every country, and so does Tarzan and Mister Macawber and Fanny Hill and Philip Marlowe. So, too, do your own friends and enemies and family members — not to mention the men and women whose faces grace the wanted posters in the post office.

Now step even further into your own experience. Close your eyes. Think of how a friend appears to you. How would you describe that person to the police? In all likelihood, your friend would come through as a "big guy," "little woman," "pretty girl," "smart-ass kid," "shabby old man," or the like.

Vague, right? Blurry. Indefinite. Less than sparkling.

Does this come through as distressingly close to some of my comments earlier on tags and labels? It should, for I confess shamelessly that elements of repetition are involved.

This time, however, our emphasis will be not on the labeling or tagging process as such, but on how best to describe such tags and labels.

What we're after is an approach — a technique, a tool — for using language, words, to make each character individual and unique and evocative of feeling.

That tool, that technique, is *specificity*.

Rule of thumb: The more specific you get, the more vivid you get.

Thus, it's not enough to speak merely of a man or a woman. What's essential is to make that man or woman different from any other; to individualize him or her to the point that he stands out unmistakably from the crowd.

How do you do this?

You downplay generalities and, instead, concentrate on the telling detail. You walk wide around words that apply to anyone: man, woman, boy, girl, fat, thin, tall, short, pretty, and the like, save as a launching pad.

Beyond that launching pad you start, of course, with the Big Picture, the dominant impression: adjective of manner, vocational noun. Then you incorporate additional tags and traits that modify it, flesh it out, as described in Chapter 4.

As you write, however, you get down to cases. Specifics.

That is, if you're talking about a man with a limp, don't let it be just any limp. Make it individual, distinctive. Perhaps the man lurches along, or drags his foot, or humps his shoulders as if each step were painful. Does he walk with a rigid, erect stance, in a manner that says he doesn't want to acknowledge his handicap? Or is his progression more that of a person who's undergone a Provo kneecap job? Or the tentative, unsteady totter in the manner often found in someone eighty years of age?

Is Character a woman—a less than fragile flower, to say the least? If so, don't be content just to call her tough, or to go through the hackneyed cigarette-tapping/lighting/snuffing out routine. Let her, instead, retrieve a can of Copenhagen from her purse and tuck a pinch of snuff beneath her upper lip. Or perhaps she wears black lipstick, or has a scorpion tattooed on her inner thigh.

These are factual details that make the person described ever so much an individual. At the same time, they draw forth a reaction, a feeling, from the reader. Yet they do so without using judgmental words, without injecting the writer's opinion into the picture in subjective phrasing. When you say, "She was a tough-looking broad," you're passing judgment on her. You're assessing her in terms of your personal prejudices. And Reader may or may not agree.

If, on the other hand, you report that "She wore a smudged T-shirt at the moment, torn to the point that her bra-less left breast was almost falling out. The shirt blazoned the slogan, 'Death from Below!' and the image of a blood-dripping knife," your reader is in a position to draw his own conclusions. If *he* wants to label her a tough-looking broad, that's an acceptable expression of his attitude. Same for "She crossed her legs. The split skirt fell away, revealing a scorpion tattooed high on the inside of her right thigh." The onus of judgment isn't on you.

Working from this principle, shall we postulate another rule of sorts, then? *In description, your goal should be to provide your readers with the raw material to enable them to draw their own conclusions.*

Reader may or may not agree with you when you say Character looks hung over. But he'll decide for himself if you say that your man looks up at you out of "bleary, bloodshot eyes" while he "scrubs shaking fingers along his stubbled jaw."

In the same way, your female lead will come through more sharply if she "runs slender fingers along the laddering in her stocking, scowling and muttering, 'Oh, shit!' as a nail snags a loose thread," rather than merely "exclaiming petulantly."

How do you find such details, such specifics to describe?

The trick here is to draw upon the images that already exist within your brain, born of your own experience. Conjure up a picture of precisely what you saw — or heard or touched or smelled or tasted. Then, link it to the feelings, good or bad, that it stimulated. Is the issue woodsmoke? Fond memories of romance around the campfire may be the concept that you're seeking. Or the image it brings may be the shock and pain of a forest fire that destroyed your mountain cabin. Is this a moment when you can't escape the driving strains and discords of Kurt Weill's *Three-Penny Opera*? What are the feelings that go with it? Search out words to describe it, capture it on paper, on a level where your reader shares the experience with you. Or, work the process in reverse. Whatever feeling you're trying to evoke, try to pin down stimuli that might tie to it.

Do you get the idea? First, in your own mind, settle on the feeling you want. But then, instead of *telling* Reader what that feeling is, walk wide around the temptation to hand him your interpretation on a platter. Instead, draw the picture in a way as to let *him* decide what it means. It's one thing to say, "He was a real con man," another to draw a picture for your reader with, "I listened. Tears glistened in Horst's eyes as he told me how the police were trying to frame him. The only trouble was, the property clerk already was sorting through old Mrs. Taggart's jewelry, reclaimed from the spare tire of Horst's car."

Such objective presentations are most effective when they concentrate on the *particular,* the *definite,* and the *concrete,* rather than the general, the vague, and the abstract.

Why? Because when you speak of the particular, it means that you're dealing with a single person, unique and special, rather than people in general. "Definite" says exact, specific — in grammar, *the* is the definite article; *a,* the indefinite. "Concrete" equals real, material — not vague or abstract.

Particular, definite, concrete formulations draw pictures in your readers' heads. Vivid pictures, especially if you bear down on things you can see and hear and smell and taste and touch. And seeing is believing, as the saying goes, for in the last analysis all our feelings spring from sensory perceptions. Tomatoes are one red, the setting sun another, blood a third; and each conjures up its own special feeling. Remember the smell of lilacs, or bacon frying, or day-old sweat, or ether? The smoothness of mink, the graininess of sand (and, in contrast, that of scouring powder), the roughness of a rasp or splintered wood? The taste of ripe Camembert cheese, and that of sharp cheddar; of chocolate and peppermint and licorice.

It will help, too, in your descriptions, if you make use as much as possible of *active* verbs as differentiated from passive.

What's an active verb? It's one that shows Character taking action, *doing* something, rather than merely existing. As in "He sat down heavily," instead of "He was sitting." (Even better, get rid of the adverb, the "heavily." Make it, for instance, "With a grunt, he sat down, clutching the old chair's arms and letting his weight go before his rump hit, so that the old chair squeaked in protest.") It just may make a more vivid picture.

(Simplicity and brevity are important in writing, but not as important as vividness.)

Beyond this, never forget that things don't have feelings; an individual person does.

A feeling is a private interpretation of data. If a thing is important, it's important to *somebody*.

Bear in mind, also, who it is who's experiencing any event you report on, the differences in what they react to. If a character describing another character weighs in at 125 pounds dripping wet, he or she will see a 250-pound woman as monstrous . . . whereas if Narrator is 400, the 250-pounder may come through as positively sylph-like. An old woman will focus on stimuli that a child or her daughter-in-law or a policeman quite possibly may ignore in favor of more personal reactions.

The old woman: "She saw the way his biceps bulged out the rolled-up sleeves. It brought back the ache to her forearm, where he'd dug in his fingers. Involuntarily, ever so slightly, she shivered."

The child: "The man's face got red and and sort of mean and he sat down on his heels. He looked blobbish that way, like one of the big clown toys that was round on the bottom and you couldn't knock it over. 'Hey, kid,' he said. His breath smelled bad."

The daughter-in-law: "Her mind kept coming back to the stubble, how it had scratched her face, her breasts. And his hands, his fingers. The way they always poked and prodded and gouged."

The veteran cop: "Automatically, he noted the way the squat stranger's left eyelid drooped till the eye was almost closed, like he was sighting a gun. The chin drew in against the chest and the shoulders hunched in a way that said he'd maybe fought pro some time or other."

Four different people, four different reactions.

Note, however, that each reaction focuses on a stimulus—in other words, there's something for the character to react to; and each gives heed to something different.

Where do you acquire all these details?

You collect them, of course. Primarily by your own, personal observation as you ask yourself what fragments of appearance and behavior indicate that a character is a wimp, or a braggart, or a bully, or a fuss-budget, or an egghead, or a slattern.

This is to say, you watch people—probably on a level you've never watched before.

In a restaurant, for example, it might be to your advantage to focus on as simple an act as coffee-drinking. Entirely apart from sugar/cream/black divisions, does everyone follow the same pattern? Who stirs and who doesn't? Who spoons the coffee and who sips—or slurps, or gulps—from the cup? Does anyone stir with a finger in the absence of a spoon, or run his tongue along the cup rim after every swallow? What happens when coffee slops into a saucer? Does the subject of your attention pour it back into the cup? Or slip a paper napkin into the saucer? Or call a waitress? Or get red-faced with irritation? And so on, *ad infinitum.*

Coffee-drinking isn't the issue, of course. Awareness is. For unless you acquire the habit of paying attention to the things people do, commonplace or funny or far out, you'll lack a vital tool for writing. What counts is development of your mind's eye, so that when you need action or bits of business you can recall some fragment you can use or distort or combine with others without making a major issue of it.

Collect incidents in the same way. The reaction of a boy in tennis shoes who kicks a prickly pear. The expression of outraged frustration on the face of a man who finds his fresh-slaughtered side of beef has been wrapped in a kerosene-soaked tarp. The revulsion and horror that goes with the discovery on entering an apartment that the friend you came to visit is three days dead and stenching.

You may even want to take advantage of the approach used by cartoonists. The trick is to mount a mirror conveniently close at hand so you can mime in it, registering whatever emotion you feel to be appropriate for the character about whom you're writing at the moment.

In so doing, remember to stay objective, factual, nonjudgmental. *Show* how the character looks and acts, and then let your readers extract whatever feelings they wish from it. Or, if you need subjective insights, let another character voice them as representing his own viewpoint: "Joe scowled. 'He's a mean-looking mother,' he grunted."

Whatever your approach, never forget that reader response will depend to a large degree on your providing Character with the right stimuli. If you want him to register anger, give him something to be angry about. Same for passion, pity, or pain.

By all means, too, be sure to relate Character to story. Never let him be like the person who insists on telling you about someone you have no involvement with and don't care about. "So what?" isn't a reaction you want to evoke.

It goes without saying, too, that your own personality and tastes will play a major role in this matter of how you write about your characters. Purple prose was a thing beloved of Poe and Lovecraft, and the sparse objective style that marked Hemingway and Hammett drew imitators not as single spies but in battalions. Trollope, in his own time, was as much a master on his front as Elmore Leonard today is on his. And I gurgle with delight at the hilarious distortions twisted on language by Robert Bloch's Lefty Feep, even though I could never so warp it myself in a thousand years.

Styles in character description change, also. When Dostoyevsky describes a character as "a diminutive, withered up old woman of sixty, with sharp malignant eyes and a sharp little nose. Her colourless, somewhat grizzled hair was thickly smeared with oil, and she wore no kerchief over it. Round her thin long neck, which looked like a hen's leg, was knotted some sort of flannel rag, and in spite of the heat, there hung flapping on her shoulders, a mangy fur cape, yellow with age,'' he's writing for an 1860's reader, not today's. And Horatio Alger's handling of Ragged Dick and Tattered Tom is unlikely to capture a mass audience in these closing years of the twentieth century.

Figures of speech—comparison, metaphor, simile, personification, and the like—are useful tools in adding color, provided they're handled with some sense of proportion. Run into the ground, on the other hand, they can render your best efforts ridiculous, as witness some of the examples cited in Bill Pronzini's mirth-provoking *Gun in Cheek.*

Words' connotations, their emotional overtones, complicate the problem. *Honky* is no more complimentary than *nigger,* and both mirror bitter feelings. Is *gay* pejorative on the same level as *queer* or *fairy*? What kind of feelings are aroused by *freak* or *freedom fighter*? Is *bad* a plaudit or an insult? How about *sharp* versus *stylish, cool* versus *hip*? Do make it your business to become ever so much aware of such, for both characters and adjectives frequently become dated.

It also will be to your advantage to listen—specifically, to listen to how characters speak, how they say the things they say, as well as to other aspects of the spoken language.

We'll take such up in "The Things They Say," our next chapter.

13

THE THINGS THEY SAY

How do you write good dialogue?
You pay as much attention to
feelings as to words.

The things a person says reflect and reveal his character. Couple his speech with that of other story people and you have dialogue, one of a writer's most useful tools for creating unique individuals, revealing relationships, building conflict, and advancing a story.

There are a variety of other reasons for a writer to use dialogue, of course. One is that, well done, it makes reading easier. It isn't as silly as it sounds. Watch the browsers at any bookstore if you don't believe me. Thumbing through the opening pages of a book, more often than not they'll pause at a broken page, one with lots of white space.

A page with dialogue, specifically.

The solid, blocky pages, heavy with copy? They'll tend to pass those by.

There are more reasons for using dialogue than easy reading, of course. A major one is drama.

Ray Palmer, my old pulp editor and mentor, put this in the simplest possible form.

"Always open with dialogue," he told me. "Why? Because when two people are talking, they have to be talking *about* something—something your readers can understand without a lot of explanation. Like for instance a fight."

Well, that may be overstating it a little, but the principle's sound. Dialogue equals people, and people talking equals some sort of interchange of information or ideas or feelings. Chitchat isn't enough. Even two lovers exchanging sweet nothings in bed is a prelude to something about to happen.

In addition, the tone of that dialogue sets a mood for the scene, establishes a feeling. Witness our two lovers with their verbal foreplay.

Note, too, that one wrong word or phrase can change that mood and lead to someone getting up and going home or to the guest room.

So. Dialogue provides both mood and information.

Often, also, it can be used to contrast the difference between what a viewpoint character thinks and what he says. Again, consider two lovers—apparent lovers, that is:

> *"I adore you, Carolyn," he said, stroking her hand gently.*
> *A nicely calculated move, it bared his wristwatch: 7:30. Desperately, he searched for some acceptable excuse to leave. He had to get to Deirdre's by eight. Yet he couldn't make it obvious. Not with Carolyn's inheritance in the balance.*

An additional dialogue value is the way it lends an air of reality to a story. The things a person says, the way he speaks, are major factors in bringing him alive on the page. It's one thing to say your heroine's rival is amoral and less than literate, another to quote a line like "So he's on the take. Who cares? A buck is a buck. He can snag my nylons anytime."

What about dialogue's individualizing function?

The words you speak, what you say and how you say it, reveal you as a particular person. If you're bookish, you talk one way; if a sports fan, another. Intelligence comes through, and so does slow-wittedness or illiteracy. The cautious person speaks with restraint, the reticent as little as possible—perhaps to the point of limiting himself to monosyllables to a great degree. Garrulousness may indicate a pulsing ego. But then again, it may not; the rush and gush of words sometimes reflect embarrassment, and any police interrogator knows the value of silence at the right moment in pushing a suspect to confess. Most bartenders and airline hostesses have been conditioned to make conversation with anyone and on any subject.

These are things a writer must think about, be aware of. If the words he puts in his story people's mouths are out of character, he'll be hard put to rise above them.

Those words should reflect such factors as sex, age, occupation, status, and background.

A grandmother speaks: "I keep everything tidy."

Her housewife daughter: "I like a neat house. But quality time together beats spick and span."

Housewife's teenage girl: "So the joint is a mess. Who cares?"

Housewife's clerk-typist friend: "I try to straighten the place up, but it gets to be a shambles."

The manager's wife: "I have this wonderful Puerto Rican woman. She keeps our house spotless."

The Puerto Rican: "All the time clean, clean. I get so—how you say?—*cansada*. Sometimes I wish I go back to San Juan."

If housewife's husband is middle management, he'll probably speak reasonably literate standard English. His mechanic may not. And his doctor quite possibly will salt his lines with medical terms totally out of range of his patients' experience. A solder has his own vocabulary, and so does a sailor, and so does a miner and a carpenter and a farmer. It also goes without saying that Maine and Mississippi and California and Colorado and the Carolinas have their private speech patterns.

(It should be noted, though, that regional differences and area dialects are fading, thanks to television, education, and military service. Outside of an occasional phrase added for color, beware of throwing in chunks of Ozark or Cajun folk speech or the like. To have one Black character describe another as a "bad dude" makes your point. To inflict a page of "Like I mean ya know I doin' skag like I ain't not ready to wig out on no crystal" on your readers is something else.)

How do learn to individualize with dialogue? The answer, of course, is that you listen, and that does mean *listen*, to people of all sorts talking in all sorts of situations insofar as you can manage it. Television and, in particular, the VCR are useful tools in this regard. By taping a program you can play chunks of dialogue that impress you over and over again until you get their pattern, their rhythm, their individualizing touches.

Beware, however, of putting too much trust in such. A TV performance is a carefully polished thing. The skill of writer, director and actors sometimes can throw you off center.

One way around this is to do some private taping with your own recorder. Hide the instrument in some place where people talk—a teachers' lounge, for example, or an office smoking area, or a garage waiting room, or by a feed store cash register—and study the results carefully.

The results may surprise you. You'll discover that people seldom talk in a straight line, and that much of what they say is fragmentary, banal, and well-nigh meaningless. There'll be a lot of what's sometimes described as pre-symbolic utterance—words designed merely to evidence non-hostility and open contact on the "Nice day, isn't it?" and "What's new?" level: "Hey, Joe." "Yo, Mack." "Wife finally let you out?"

Men talk differently when there are no women present than when there are. So do women when there are no men. Teenagers hardly speak to each other in the same language they use around parents or other adults. Ditto for Blacks, druggies, doctors, soldiers—just about any group you can name. If you're presenting characters from such a category, they must speak with the flavor of their "in" patois. But beware long, unreadable passages of word-for-word phonetic transcription. As pointed out before, such will tend to lose readers.

However intrigued with such you are, however, don't ever forget to assign your people individual tags of speech, special phrases and patterns and topics that help identify them for your readers. (Did I say topics? Yes. A character who never can forget the Mets or Dodgers or his beloved '66 Chevy is as clearly labeled as if he spoke Swahili.)

Listening to people, you'll encounter endless empty conversations—". . . and then I said, and then he said"—that merely fill time. (This world is full of people who can't stand silence.)

All this helps you to grasp the flavor of speech. But beware of using it as more than spice when you write dialogue. So far as your story's concerned, it's "dead time"—waste space on the page that could be put to better advantage advancing your story.

Unless, that is, your object is to show how vapid and boring a particular character is. And even then, more than a little may prove too much. Putting readers to sleep is a cardinal sin!

On the other side of the coin, there are times in any story when you need what amounts to filler, in order to expand a moment of tension. Or perhaps you must provide Villain with some sort of cover to distract Hero while the bomb is planted or the files stolen, so you send in Villain's accomplice to hold Hero away from the action with chains of banality while Reader, who knows about the bomb or the robbery, is jumping up and down with panic-bred suspense.

Bear in mind, however, that the key to including empty words is to establish the time pressure and potentiality for disaster *before* you throw in meaningless, time-wasting dialogue which slows the hero.

Whatever the pattern you're trying to achieve, practice is your key to improvement. To learn to write good dialogue, write dialogue endlessly. Then commandeer friends to read it back into a tape recorder. Inevitably, no matter how you cringe at the result, the work will sharpen your lines.

What about the relation between story and dialogue?

Your story moves from one state of affairs and state of emotion to another state of affairs and state of emotion—in other words, from beginning to end. And from beginning to end it's a continuing process and reflection of change—specifically, the change of your character's state of mind and situation.

Each scene, each episode, must reflect this. It must play a role in affecting this change.

As an important component of said change, ever and always dialogue must advance the plot.

How do you make dialogue do this advancing? By having it give the reader information needed to understand what's happening.

In providing that information, most speeches should be designed to influence another character's attitude or behavior.

It also will help if this data comes in bits and pieces, rather than indigestible chunks:

"Where could she have gone?"
"The bar, probably."
"Thanks a lot. I doubt there's more than a hundred bars in town."
"Not on Denton Street."
"Denton Street! My God, she couldn't have gone there."
"It's Eddy's turf."
"Heimlich's too! And if he gets hold of her—"
"Oh, Lord, I read you! We've got to move."
"Like fast."
They hit the door running.

You understand, it would have been simple enough to say, "There are a lot of bars in town, but probably she's gone to one of the ones down on Denton Street. That's Eddy's turf. The only trouble is, Heimlich's moving in there too. And if he gets hold of her — well, we'd better move fast." But it wouldn't have been as effective. Short speeches, sentence fragments, broken phrases read faster and hold audience interest tighter most of the time.

It's vital, too, that in addition to conveying information, good dialogue should reveal and build emotion. It's not just weather talk, it's goal-oriented. The people who are talking want something: in the example above, to find the girl.

Further, finding her is important, and there's an implied time factor to drive the searchers.

You may even come to feel that it's not a bad idea to try, wherever possible, to center your dialogue around a character's efforts to accomplish something, change something. Then let Character 2, to whom he's speaking, either agree or disagree, be set up to help or hinder.

If Character 2 agrees, hold down the bit. Why? Because dialogue of agreement is dull. If he disagrees, the passage probably calls for greater development because it reflects conflict, and conflict with its potentiality of failure for Character 1 evokes emotion.

Does this mean that dialogue must always center around action scenes? No. The issue is merely that, as mentioned before, most speeches should be designed to influence someone's attitude or behavior:

> "*It's a good job,*" *he said.* "*I could go a million years and never get a better chance. Just because it means a move —*"
>
> "*I know, John. Only . . .*"
>
> "*Only — ?*"
>
> "*Mother.*"
>
> "*Stell, we can't tie our lives to her forever.*"
>
> "*But her home, her church, her friends. They mean so much to her. She'd be lost without them.*"
>
> "*Stell, we stay here with me in a dead-end job and our own lives are lost. Don't they count too?*"
>
> "*Please, John. Can't we at least think it over?*"
>
> "*All right, all right. We'll think it over.*"

Again, conflict. But a different kind of conflict. On a lower level at the moment, it paves the way for something more intense later on.

Note, too, how situation influences speech pattern. Urgent moments, bits loaded with action and tension, tend to be characterized by short words, short sentences, short speeches. An episode in which characters reflect, debate, try to decide what to do or to review past incidents, move more slowly and draw forth longer, more thoughtful speeches.

So there you have it where dialogue's concerned: By the words your people say and the manner in which they say them, it should characterize and individualize them . . . give information to advance the plot . . . reveal and build the emotion that galvanizes the story.

Beyond that, always strive for the *provocative* line. Hunt for at least occasional new, fresh, original ways for your characters to say whatever it is they have to say. In their proper places, slang, colorful analogies, personification, and the like can prove very effective.

How do you find the provocative line? Write whatever dull clichés come handy, then go back and rework. "Complex" may then become "as tangled up as a meatball in a can of spaghetti." "Jumpy" is reworked to "jerking like a crawdad on a hook" or "wriggling like a barefoot boy on hot cement."

Which is fine within limits. Just don't carry it so far that your readers label it as straining for effect.

Bear in mind also that only scientists and others trained to speak in facts do so. Others filter information through their emotional reactions. Most people think and talk more in terms of "great," "awful," "dumb," "But, Mother, everyone's doing it," "I mean, it was the longest speech I ever heard," "Hah, I wasn't scared, but he was *big*!" And ask any policeman how precise the drivers in a fender-bender are in their accounts of the accident!

Never forget as you write dialogue that the situation—the state of affairs, and the state of mind of your characters—are changing continually as your story progresses. Your story people's emotions are in flux. Their speeches should reflect this.

Try to keep reticence as common in dialogue as it is in life. Few of us will tell a woman how ugly she is save in a rage, nor lecture her husband on how badly brought up their children are. A well-bred man who flaunts his wealth shows poor taste, and so does a woman who brags about her promotion, or any of a hundred other deviations from propriety. Nor do we reveal intimate or embarrassing moments easily. Our pattern, if we're going to talk at all about such, is to divulge just a little, tentatively . . . wait for a reaction . . . then tell a little more.

Bad taste, bad manners, and rudeness have their place, however. Given the right character and situation, they may come through with truly shocking shock value.

Where do you use dialogue? In general, you may find it most effective when it reflects a certain tension, great or small, in at least one character. Thus, he's likely to resort to it to break the ice when he meets someone new or feels nervous in a social situation. When he has a goal, wants something, or seeks to win information dialogue is a device to help him get it. In moments of crisis he may lose control and lash out at opponents or bystanders.

Just *don't* use it merely to fill space or substitute for thinking through your plot!

How much dialogue should you include?

That depends on your story, of course. But remember what I said earlier about the value of white space and broken pages in helping to catch reader attention.

And don't be tempted to try for the story told 100 percent in dialogue or totally without it. They're literary stunts and not worth your time as a real writer.

How do you make the speeches in a dialogue episode hang together? In general, the trick is to let each one acknowledge the one ahead of it.

Sometimes, the first speech may be a question, the second an answer:

> *"Where did you go?"*
> *"Oh, downtown and around."*

Sometimes the linkage is a repetition:

> *"I'm sorry, but I simply haven't got the money."*
> *"You haven't got the money? What happened to it?"*

An "empty" word or phrase may serve as a bridge:

> *"I hate to make a move this way."*

"I know, I know. But there's Edna's sister to consider."

An action often may take the place of words in any conversation:

"Sarah, I simply can't understand you."
Sarah turned away as if Cecile hadn't even spoken. In wordless silence she looked out across the hills, the harbor.

There are all sorts of continuity devices such as these. Simply check the dialogue passages in any book or magazine till you become familiar with them, then practice using them in your own work. Soon they'll become second nature to you.

Remember, too, that silence can be golden, as in the case of Sarah, above, if someone doesn't want to discuss a matter further. And if you still want to introduce the information Character walked away from, you can always have another person hazard a guess as to what Character thought or felt.

Finally, when it dawns on you that a dialogue sequence has bogged down, don't despair. Length quite possibly is the issue. Go back over the passage again and cut, condense, intensify, tighten. Believe me, another day will prove it was worth the effort.

Beyond dialogue, there's another aspect of characterization every writer should consider: how to handle your people in stories of different lengths and genres, as well as in media other than the printed page.

Our next chapter, "Variations on a Theme," surveys it.

14

VARIATIONS ON A THEME

*How do you treat characters in the
various lengths, media, and genres?
You design your people to
fit your market.*

So how do you build a character to fit a specific length, genre, or medium?

Length, first. What are the special problems you face in creating a character for each of the various specialties?

THE SHORT STORY

Space—wordage—is the primary issue in the short story. The shorter your story, the more limited your presentation of your character must be.

Samuel Armstrong, for example, may live in a variety of worlds. In one, it's Sam and wife, in another Sam and children, in a third Sam and aging mother . . . Sam and job, hobbies, religion, recreations, dreams, intellectual interests—the list goes on and on.

But you can't explore them all in a short story. Even though you make passing reference to other phases of his life, space limitations demand that you spotlight one—his concern with his wife's increasing coldness or his drug-addicted teen-age son, his involvement with a mistress, his worries about whether he'll be passed over for promotion, his nervousness over the badgering and sniping by Ed Sims at the next desk, his secret fears that the spurts of pounding in his chest foreshadow early death of a heart attack like the ones which claimed his grandfather and father.

Arbitrarily, we'll pick one of Sam's problems to spotlight: the fact that he's just discovered his son is heavy into drugs.

But selecting one of Sam's problems on which to focus is only your first step. Now you must decide how to present him.

Since this is to be a short story, you're again space limited.

Odds are you'll have to hold your handling down to the dominant impression, dominant attitude, and goal or purpose level. Perhaps we'll see Sam as an uptight, security-oriented, middle-bracket executive whose dominant attitude is caution, not rocking the boat. Though he's largely preoccupied with business, he has a compulsive love of family and aches because his duty-born determination to get his son off drugs makes them antagonists too often. His goal at the moment is to force his already hostile wife to recognize that their son has a drug problem and agree to place the boy in a treatment center.

This goal, note, is one that can be brought into focus quickly, then carried through to a climax and conclusion in two or three scenes. While it *could* be developed to novel length, it also can be held down to short story level.

At this point, however, Sam remains physically nebulous. You're going to have to provide him with a body, tags, traits—specific items to give him color and make him recognizable, likable.

Let's say he's cast in a nondescript corporate mold. His only distinguishing characteristics are his increasingly bald head, the fact that he ponders a lot—considering whatever problem is at hand through narrowed eyes, and that he habitually wears a scarab stickpin he inherited from his father. It's out of style, of course, and his insolent son taunts him with the nickname "Bug" in moments of irritation. Sam doesn't like that, but tells himself that Son will outgrow such nonsense. Meanwhile, to make an issue of it will only escalate their conflict. The drug thing is what's crucial.

Do you see how this works? We've given Sam the potential to be a full-blown, complex character. But because this is a short story we've held him within narrow limits, selecting a single specific emotional danger for him to deal with (though others may of course be mentioned in order to give an illusion of depth), plus labels and a goal.

And of course the picture we've drawn here is sketchy indeed. If you were actually writing the story, you'd need to think it through in a lot more detail.

THE LONG STORY

What about characterization in the long story—the novelette, the novella, the novel?

The key fact here is that you have extra wordage available, more room to move around where both the situation and your story people are concerned.

That means you may describe said people in more detail . . . explore their thoughts and feelings and relationships in greater depth. They may grow and take on new dimensions.

On the other hand—and this is a point too often forgotten in college literature classes—you don't *have* to make them more complex if you don't want to. Any number of long stories have been written in which the characters—and that includes the protagonist—remain simple and static. You can hardly class James Bond or Mike Hammer or Tarzan or Superman as failures.

But let's say you do want to delve more deeply into your people. What are the factors to consider?

Time, space, number of characters, and viewpoint, it seems to me, are the salient issues.

Where timespan ordinarily is held to a minimum in the typical genre novel, it may expand to cover generations in other types. This means that structure often will, of necessity, be episodic. In order to move through a long span of years, you'll be forced to focus on chosen key moments or periods. In each, you'll probably develop the episode as if it were a separate story, building in the familiar scene/sequel pattern. The days or months or years between segments will be bridged with narration, *telling* what happened (in emotionalized terms, most likely), as contrasted with dramatization, the *showing* of what happens that you offer within episodes.

A word of narration. A valuable tool indeed, you can use it to expand or contract presentation as desired, leaping across centuries in a sentence or drawing a picture of a time or place that goes on for pages. Well handled, it enables you to slant a portrayal so readers love or hate a person or a situation.

Because narration summarizes, however, it lacks the excitement dramatization brings. And since it represents the author telling, it may or may not be believable.

Back to the matter of extended timespan. Ordinarily, such brings with it a need for more characters than in the simple, single-problem-oriented genre novel. Which means that you'll have to conceive, conceptualize, and create said people, balancing them against those already in the story framework.

Further, these characters must reflect their place and period.

Attitudes of English Roundheads clashed with those of the Cavaliers. Chinese in the California goldfields mirrored one state of mind; those who made the Long March with Mao, another. The Irish immigrant, in his day, was disdained, and so was the Jew and the Italian, and the Appalachian poor white in Chicago in the sixties. The coal fields and the vineyards breed different attitudes. Anachronisms must be checked out, and so must speech patterns and dress and religious beliefs and racial prejudices and women's place in the family constellation.

Which means that you, author of a novel with breadth and sweep, have your research cut out for you, and it won't necessarily be quick or easy. Invariably, some key background detail can't be uncovered, and work is stymied. I've known any number of writers who spent a year or more just digging, before they ever sat down at the typewriter or word processor.

Unless you're determined to be truly scholarly, a rather obvious trick often will speed up research, however. Simply take a solid volume or two related to your subject and, when you need color detail, draw it from this source, rather than spend endless hours searching out a particular fragment. Thus, if you write mysteries, you may place great reliance on such books as LeMoyne Snyder's old but still valuable *Homicide Investigation,* Charles Swanson's *Criminal Investigation,* Phil and Karen McArdle's *Fatal Fascination,* or Stanton Samenow's *Inside the Criminal Mind.* Down the line you're likely to accumulate a fairly extensive shelf on murder and related subjects. But for practical working purposes, picking items from two or three books can stand you in very good stead.

Remember, too, that in any story, short or long, we're dealing with emotion as the key dynamic. So for each of the characters you bring to life in new episodes, you must devise emotional involvements in keeping with time/place/situation that build/contrast/clash with those of your other people, just as if you were constructing a new story.

There'll also be the issue of viewpoint to complicate things. Through whose eyes will each episode be seen? Believe me, it can be a headache. But in a long book, some change is well-nigh essential. To make it more complicated, each viewpoint character calls for different handling. Certainly there must be contrast between them, and that means more digging, more research.

Finally, what about space, geography? A panoramic war novel

or a rich, far-ranging life story like Robert L. Duncan's *China Dawn* will call for time-and-place research to fit your actors for their roles. When Jerry Pournelle and Larry Niven wrote their famous *The Mote in God's Eye,* they created not only an imaginary world, but an entire universe.

Even when you're dealing with a shorter timespan—a cradle-to-grave biography, for instance—be prepared for emotional complexities. In any life, you're confronted with the fact that a life moves through a series of emotional strata.

Thus, a child's focus may be on tensions growing from the demands of a father, a mother, or a sibling. And although conscious memory of these may pass, their emotional residue remains for years to influence Character's thoughts, attitudes, and feelings.

The early teens quite possibly brings a zeroing in on adventure, whether it be via sports or street gangs or school rivalries. Late teens see sex take the spotlight. Young adulthood brings concentration on career or marriage. And so on.

In other words, such a novel is episodic, but on a different level than the generational.

In all the long, passage-of-time/display-of-character books, you work in episodic units, jumping from episode to episode or linking episodes with narration. But within each episode, you still build with scene and sequel. They remain your foundation stones.

Since you have more space to fill in the long story, more words to play with, you can have more characters, make them more complex, perhaps even change viewpoint. But you still start from the fundamentals of dominant impression, dominant attitude, and purpose.

Don't feel obliged to lengthen your cast or complicate your people, however. Many of the most memorable characters in fiction are the next thing to stick figures. Consider Cinderella, Romeo, Tom Sawyer or, for that matter, Frankenstein. Their creators did very nicely, if you please.

THE CATEGORY CHARACTER

The category or genre book is a novel aimed at readers with particular tastes, particular interests. They know what they enjoy reading and they buy it. Publishers, in turn, being sales and profit oriented, are more than happy to supply the desired volumes.

The so-called categories range from romance and mystery to science fiction, western, horror, and adventure. Each of these major categories breaks down into sub-clusters. Harlequin romance groupings in one set of recent guidelines included "Harlequin Presents," "Harlequin Temptation," "Harlequin American Romance," "Harlequin Romantic Intrigue," and several others, each aimed at a particular reader public. In science fiction, one covey of fans insists on so-called "hard" science fiction—that is, fiction based on extrapolation from known physical science. Others like their stories social science-oriented, or prefer fantasy, "sword and sorcery," etc. Mystery readers may demand straight detective, "hard-boiled," "police procedural," "private eye," "cozy," or espionage. And so it goes, category by category.

Since a prime characteristic of all these genres is that their readers know what they want, you need to know too if you plan to write in the field. Indeed, your best bet is to pick an area in which you yourself are a fan and have read widely, so the implicit rules and assumptions, the things fans take for granted, are already built into your head.

That this will influence your choice and development of characters goes without saying, especially if you write romance. Thus, Silhouette's guidelines described the heroine of its "Intimate Moments" series as "a sympathetic character. Independent, intelligent and strongwilled, she should also be emotionally vulnerable. Though she may find herself in circumstances unfamiliar to most readers, she reacts to them in a familiar and believable way." Candlelight Romances says its heroine "should have been born in the United States and preferably raised there. Between twenty-two and twenty-eight years old, she has *at least* a high school education and preferably college. She should have a job which she enjoys with aspirations toward a high position or level of achievement . . ."

One word of warning: Category book requirements are continually changing. Picking up a stack of old paperbacks to study can give you a dangerously wrong impression of where the market stands today. If you want to write for a category market, study only current guidelines or the most recent releases.

And beyond this? The secret is to create good characters, likable characters, self-consistent/predictable characters, believable characters. By and large they'll be interesting, colorful people who don't take trouble lying down. Or, as one of my favorite editors once told me, "I want heroines, not victims!"

THE RADIO CHARACTER

Although radio no longer offers much of a market, that may not be the case for long. Taped fiction is coming up fast, with adaptations from both novels and short stories now being readied. A growing enclave of commuters, joggers, and just passive "readers" is opening to them.

From the writer's standpoint, a character on radio — or tape — remains a character. Dynamically he or she is the same as in print, even though most of the time in all likelihood you're going to have to simplify the character to fit the medium. To that end, concentrate on dominant impression (noun of vocation, adjective of manner), dominant attitude, and goal/purpose. Where presentation is concerned, only technical details change.

Specifically:

1. Your audience can't see your people, only hear them.
2. Getting inside a character on tape is going to be more difficult than it is in print.

Let's begin with Roadblock No. 1. Since you're denied the visual element by the medium, you have to draw pictures of your people in *sound.*

How do you do this?

To begin with, the announcer is a great help. He can fill the listener in on time, place, and situation.

> ANNOUNCER:
> It's a quiet evening in Rockville . . . especially quiet in the alley behind the real estate office. Ed and Olly are waiting in the shadows for the beat cop to check the door.

Identity is something else again. You may designate one line for Ed, another for Olly, but how is Listener to know which is which? The answer is, he won't — not unless early on you have one refer to the other by name:

ED:
Get back here, Olly! You want that cop to see you?

OLLY:
Aw, cool it, Ed. We'll hear him before he turns in.

And of course it wouldn't hurt to give each character a verbal tag or two:

ED:
What I'm doing in this hick burg is more than I can figure.
New York, New York—that's my town!

OLLY:
(mimicking) New York, New York. That's all you talk about. Me, I'll take Kansas.

Beyond obvious things like this, the trick is to create images—sound supplemented, where possible—with the things your people say. It's not enough to have Ed cross to the desk where the manager keeps the safe combination, because radio listeners can't see the action. Rather, you've got to translate it into audible words.

ED:
The combination, Olly! Get the combination!

OLLY:
Which desk?

ED:
The big one, dummy, the boss's.

Sound now takes over—the sound of Olly's footsteps, then the scrape of a drawer opening, then the rattle of shuffling papers.

OLLY:
What's it look like? This is just a bunch of papers.

Well, this is supposed to be a text on character, not radio writing. But you get the idea.

In developing your characters, beyond the things they themselves say, the things other characters say about them will help you give them added dimension. To this end, however, you need to give your primary people something to do for their fellows to talk about. What a character does defines him, so you devise bits, incidents, and situations that give him an opportunity to behave in character on a level that your audience can hear.

Furthermore, "what he does" should have its origins in emotion, since that's the bedrock on which your story rests.

> ED:
> You think I'm going to buy that? Booze is no excuse.
>
> SOUND: Bottle smashing.
>
> ED:
> To hell with you!
>
> SOUND: Door slamming.

Yes, radio can capture emotion. A sob, a snarl, a laugh, a whisper will translate emotion into sound.

What about the second roadblock we mentioned above: the problem of getting inside a character?

Individual thoughts, stream of consciousness or the like can be achieved by a variety of technical tricks. One of the most common tricks is the use of an echo or filter microphone, both of which distort sound to create special effects in radio drama.

> ED:
> Get back here, Olly!
>
> (ECHO MIKE) My god, how did I ever get hooked up with this dodo? But I've got to get into that safe!

Similarly, a narrator may be used to reveal information not normally put in actual dialogue. It also saves time.

> NARRATOR:
> Lord knows Ed didn't want to crack that safe, but it was Julie's neck for sure if he didn't. Only he couldn't let Olly know that. Olly had to think he was just after the dough.

The point I hope I'm making here is that radio has its limitations where character presentation is concerned. But given a bit of imagination and persistence, you probably can work out a satisfactory handling.

THE STAGE CHARACTER

What about characterization in the theatre?

A stage play gives you both sight and sound to work with where your people are concerned. But this doesn't free you quite as much as you might imagine.

To begin with, you have to use dialogue to provide information on anything that happens offstage. And it's every bit as hard—maybe more so—to get inside the head of a character in a stage play as it is to invade the thoughts and feelings of one designed for radio. Narrators, Greek choruses, and asides to the audience are out of style and blackouts in the "Waiting for Lefty" mode tend to seem artificial—as they are. So most often you're left with the task of revealing everything in action and dialogue (primarily dialogue), or else devising tricks to surmount the limitations.

In addition, you face the problem that presentation will be "broad"—that is, action must be exaggerated enough to reach a relatively distant audience.

Also, the proscenium arch holds the scene of action to a relatively small area and limits the action itself. And arena staging has its own problems.

Nor are actors and directors always an unadulterated joy to work with. Both tend to change your lines to suit their own ideas, even though the Dramatists Guild says you call the shots. In consequence, you have no choice but to attempt to design a so-called "actor-proof" play—one that will bring down the house no matter how clumsily presented.

Yes, it can be done, but it isn't easy. The answer, insofar as there is one, is to create characters the audience can believe in and cheer for, caught up in a situation that freezes said audience in its seats.

In other words, create men and women who care desperately about something that's threatened and will fight to get or keep it. In comedy as well as drama? Yes, and maybe even more so.

This book gives the fundamentals of how to create such people. To adapt them to the stage is a matter of understanding the theatre as well as writing, however. To that end, immerse yourself in theatre as fan, actor, stagehand — watching plays, reading plays, writing plays without number until one hits.

THE FILM/TV CHARACTER

Where characterization for film and television is concerned, the big plus is that it isn't limited by the proscenium arch, as is the stage. There is no "offstage," since the camera can jump anywhere, whether it's next door or to Kenya or on the moon.

In addition, clothes and sets help to characterize your people.

Film also has the tremendous advantage of the closeup. That is, the camera can fill the screen with any fragment of action or expression desired, whether it be a postage stamp upside down on a letter, a shot of eyes going wide with panic, or a breath sucked in in a manner that leaves no doubt of the character's passion. Attention can be focused on a watchface or a ring or a pistol in a hip pocket without need of action or dialogue. There is the problem of revealing thoughts or bringing the past into the present, but flashbacks and other similar devices can take at least acceptable care of that.

Remember John Wayne's insightful comment that in film, actors react rather than act. And study of a few movies or TV episodes will show you that by the very nature of the medium actors perform actions more than they seem to think. This performance is a reaction resulting from a thought, and it interests audiences more than does the thought itself.

Indeed, the worst aspect of film/TV may be that its great strength lies in its very capacity for showing action. In consequence, it tends to concentrate on fights, cataclysms, and car chases. The quiet and the thoughtful too often are ignored or relegated to talking heads.

For the writer, this means that he ordinarily has little future in the field unless he turns out strongly plotted "action stuff." If that's to his taste, he may have a career. If it isn't, perhaps he's better off with print.

Be that as it may, a writer still wants to write, which makes characters his business.

Sometimes those characters may be in the past or future, or aspects of present society with which the writer is unfamiliar.

That poses problems, but they can be solved. So, let's take a look at them in the next chapter, "The Character Out of Time."

15

THE CHARACTER OUT OF TIME

How do you get people to read about characters in unfamiliar worlds? You provide emotional insight into the world and individuals involved.

This chapter concerns characters who live in worlds separate from our own, milieus that each have their own peculiarities and uniquenesses.

As mentioned briefly in Chapter 14, those separate worlds, those milieus, shape the characters who live in them. If you don't have a grasp of the world you focus on, it means that you may — probably will — fail to understand the characters also, for often they play by rules different than those we ordinarily assume.

Your readers, in turn, must know and understand the world in which any given story takes place in order for that story to be effective. You the writer are the person who, with the images and insights you paint with words, helps them to attain that understanding. Failure to make the story world and its special rules clear to readers automatically limits you to the shoot-'em-up level of fiction.

Even an unfamiliar geography may change the rules, the circumstances. The adventure set in Timor or Patagonia calls for knowledge of those places. Too many service veterans and travelers have seen the landscape and the culture for you to get away with faking.

I term the people who populate special story worlds characters out of time. They fall into three categories: those from the past (that is, history); those from the future, as in science fiction; and those who fall into what I call the "not-you" contemporary, the groups whose lifestyles are outside your ken, even though you may see and work with them every day.

While the members of each of these groups certainly are as

human as any other story people, dealing with them frequently involves special problems, for to make past, future, or not-you contemporary characters effective, you must fit their attitudes and responses to their milieus, the world or society in which they live.

HISTORICAL CHARACTERS

To create a solid character from the past, you first need to know the particular world through which Character moves, and the pluses and minuses that go with it.

To that end, you must find out what's *different* about it, beyond the beards, the armament, the funny-looking clothes. It's not necessarily necessary that you be aware of who was king or what wars were fought or won or lost. Buy you *must* have an awareness of Character's goals, attitudes, and feelings and how they fit into the patterns, beliefs, and thinking of the society in which he's going to play his role.

Thus, if your story is set in a society that thinks of women only as property, your approach and your handling of your heroine — and your hero too — will be different than it would be if the society were one that believes in romantic love. If your hero's occupation is limited by guilds or class restrictions, his skills, status, and income won't be the same as if his world were one in which he has the vocational freedom of the America's nineteenth-century frontier. If his culture holds him down because he's not of noble birth, he can't function in the same way as if he were a pirate on the Spanish Main.

Similarly, attitudes in France will be different than those in Japan. Behavior will follow one pattern in Russia in the 1700s, another today. And so on.

The important thing to remember in any case is that while facts are ever so important, the feelings they engender are what make your story go. Your goal is to figure out how Character thinks, as a result of his situation. How does he see things? What are his feelings and ideas about the prevailing state of affairs? And how does he behave in view of said ideas, as contrasted with the action a man or woman of today might take?

Take a simple and obvious case in point, a xenophobic society where inordinate fear of or dislike for foreigners or strangers is the rule. We saw this in our own country, when each wave of immigration brought a new crop of prejudices and hostilities. The Irish, for example, in their day were the victims of discrimination on every level. The Jews, the Italians, the East Europeans, each suffered in their turn. Today we still see more than vestiges of leftover antagonism focused on Blacks and Hispanics. Further, all through history xenophobia has played a major role in determining who's permitted to marry whom, what jobs are available to what groups, and the pecking order that determines who's to be at the top or bottom of the communal totem pole.

That this affects fiction goes without saying. From Walter Scott's *Ivanhoe* to Sholem Asch's *East River* to John Jake's *North and South* to Janet Dailey's *Calder* books, you're dealing with cultural patterns with which many readers are unfamiliar. To reach them, you're going to have to present these patterns, and the emotions and attitudes involved, in terms that "sell" them to your audience.

Even more disruptive to our conceptions is the cultural situation that condemns the individual who rises above the group, as in the case of Latin attitudes in some areas even today. There, adding a room to your home may arouse such antagonism that your neighbors will come in the night to burn it up or tear it down. Among some American Indian tribes, an honored person gives lavish gifts to guests at a celebration as a means of equalizing wealth.

Do you need to drag cultural patterns in by the heels? Not at all. What's important is how your characters feel about them, how they react to them, and the kinships or conflicts that spring from them.

Indeed, you may need no more than a few lines that indicate a character's awareness of our attitude on a matter. But those few lines can make a difference, insofar as they add to your story's and your character's dimension.

Is your story set in Victorian England? If the picture in your mind's eye is limited to the popular image of the period as one of stiff-necked propriety, you open your range of character portrayal, potential conflicts, and story complications vastly when you broaden your vision to view a panorama that includes music halls, the secret vices of the rich, the thriving underworld, and its beggars and wanderers, cracksmen and footpads, whores and wastrels. Charles Dickens worked wonders with such.

But remember: Ever and always, you must fit your characters' thinking and feelings into the panorama, while at the same time you create understanding of and empathy with it in your readers.

How do you uncover the information you need? You look it up. You dig it out.

Don't let this scare you off. A book or two on sociology, cultural anthropology, and social history will give you a good start on the things you need to know. These will lead you to others that fit your special needs. In the course of your poking, you'll also pick up data on everything from cabbages to kings. Take advantage of it to keep an eye out for details that provide you with sensory perceptions. The drafts that whip flames about in a castle fireplace and blow out candles are a good example. Same for the feel of a horsehair couch, the unfamiliar smoothness of silk to a traveler in the Orient, the smells of spices or woodsmoke, the distortion of balance that comes with riding on a donkey or camel, the torment of flea bites, the taste of haggis or squid or buffalo tongue. One and all, they give you bits to help bring your characters to life and to reveal traits that define them—we still remember the princess so sensitive that she couldn't sleep because there was a pea under the mattress.

But such fragments are only a bonus. The feelings and attitudes that spring from environment are your primary target.

That means it's your privilege to scan and be selective. You're not going to have to pass a college test at the end of your reading. Make notes on the bits that strike you as valuable or add color. Ignore the rest.

Search, particularly, for works that describe life in your place or period. Journals, diaries, or autobiographies may prove excellent sources. When I was writing westerns—a field in which there's a whole library of works—I soon discovered that Everett Dick's *The Sod House Frontier,* Carl Coke Rister's *Southern Plainsmen,* Foster-Harris's *The Look of the Old West* and an 1897 Sears & Roebuck catalog solved my problem very nicely most of the time. Count on it—a few hours, a few books, and you'll be off and running!

Don't limit yourself to research in books, however. If your story takes place within the past couple of hundred years, you may find much valuable material in newspapers and magazines of the period about which you're writing. Museums often will become treasure houses for you. So may historical societies. A drama school costume teacher may prove an asset beyond imagining if you remember that the issue is how a garment felt to the person wearing it, not just how it looked. And James M. Cain speaks of going over court transcripts of the Civil War period in search of authentic speech patterns.

(I'll warn you yet again, though: Many of you are going to be trapped by your material. That is, some of the items you find will fascinate you to the point that in spite of yourselves you go on and on and become scholars without portfolio. That's what happened to me, at least, with the result that any day now we may have to move into a tent on the front lawn because books have taken over the house.)

But enough of history, or at least history as we normally think of it. It's time we moved on to the years, centuries, and eons ahead . . . the worlds of science fiction and what might be termed "future history."

FUTURE HISTORY

Here, let me recommend a book by William F. Noland and George Clayton Johnson. It's titled *Logan's Run*. It also was made into a highly successful film.

The story draws a devastatingly realistic picture of a future world. Overpopulation is its problem; the solution, a law that decrees death by painless sleep as soon as a person reaches age twenty-one. In consequence, with the dread of impending "sleep" forever looming, life is one long, furious pursuit of pleasure as each individual tries to cram as much sensual stimulation as possible into the too-short years before the time-measuring "flower" in his or her palm turns black.

The hero, Logan, in turn, is one of the officers whose duty it is to enforce the death rule. But when his own palm-flower begins to blacken, he can't accept the thought of oblivion. He becomes one of those who, rebelling, flee their fate—a "runner," in the jargon of the period.

It's a fascinating premise, and the "run" that follows is exciting indeed. For our purposes here, however, the key point is that the Nolan and Johnson story world is based on believable sociological projection, an extrapolation which readers can believe. Or if you want to go even further, consider Neal Barrett Jr.'s *Through Darkest America*, with its virtually surrealistic picture of post-World War

III life. The message: To create a solid character in future time, just as in history, you first need to conceptualize a unique world with intriguing problems for him to live in.

Next question: What kind of men and woman populate this world? What have the changes in environment and life done to them? Even today, conditioning and behavior modification and genetic engineering are closing in on us. How will they reshape the human animal? Will the computer replace thinking and so-called artificial intelligence take over? Are machines with personality in command? Will electrical or chemical stimulation of selected areas of the brain make possible what one writer has referred to as "unbearable pleasure, infinitely prolonged," and if it does, what effect will it have on society? What feelings and fears and attitudes do you foresee? Is "free will" ever actually free? Has humankind, in your story, gone forward into some sort of nirvana, or back into the pre-industrial world? When does education become brainwashing? What about brain grafts? In the past, we've always assumed that fictional characters have human form, but is this necessarily so? May shared mental activities come to pass? Telepathy? Clairvoyance? Teleportation? May man's goals change and new outlets for individualism be substituted for those we know? What about the pre-programming of personality and individuality?

Clearly, these days, not even the sky's the limit. But whatever world we create, we still come back to the principle laid down when we discussed the character from history. Regardless of the period or conditions about which you write, it's essential that you know the implicit or explicit ground rules of your character's society, his world, because Character's attitudes and feelings must reflect the thinking and attitudes of his time and place. Books like George Orwell's *1984,* Alfred Bester's *The Demolished Man,* and C. J. Cherryh's *Cyteen* will give you an idea of what I mean.

Here, since we're dealing with tomorrow . . . how do you create a future world?

If you're a science fiction buff (and odds are that you are, if you're contemplating a story laid in the future) you've probably got a pretty good idea of that from your prior reading in the field.

Just as in past-history work, you have a volume of existing material to help you—Brian Stableford's *Future Man,* for example; Gene Bylinsky's *Life in Darwin's Universe*; Peter Nichols's *Science Fiction Encyclopedia* and *The Science in Science Fiction*; Robert

Forward's *Future Magic;* John Taylor's *The Shape of Minds to Come,* and ever so many others. Couple such with the convolutions and warpings of your own imagination and you're bound to come up with something fascinating.

One word of caution: While you've created a new world in your own eyes, to your characters it's work-a-day familiar, so don't slip into the error of having them show too great a fascination with the technology and social patterns that have developed.

THE NOT-YOU CONTEMPORARY

This segment concerns contemporary characters.

Many of such characters may be just like you: the same sex, the same age, the same background, the same occupation, the same social groups. With these you need no help.

Others, however, on one level or another, operate by different standards. Each in his own way, they pledge allegiance to alien groups and live in separate worlds.

Why? Because their attitudes are different.

Not just their attitudes, either. Their hopes and ambitions, too, may be on an unfamiliar level. Their moral code. Their priorities. Their thinking. Their emotional reactions. Their feelings.

Especially their feelings. Emotion undergirds all the other factors.

If you eliminate these people when you cast your stories and only write about men and women wholly like you, you limit the scope and interest of your work. Perhaps drastically.

That's a luxury most of us can't afford.

Because this is so, you need to research these people so like, yet unlike you, just as you would someone out of history or the future. You can't assume that a character from a university background will think and behave the same way a character from a sharecropper's shack will. You just don't dare to take it for granted that the views of a fifty-year-old on sexual conduct will duplicate those of a seventeen-year-old or a thirty-year-old. Nor will such an individual's ideas necessarily prove consistent. A professional bank robber may have one attitude towards his trade, another where adultery or lying is concerned.

If you don't recognize this and have a depth of insight into a given character's private world, you'll have difficulty grasping that different players play by different rules, and those rules may be different than those we ordinarily assume.

You're contemporary, right? Well-geared to our present world in all respects?

Or are you? Can you get inside the head of, for example, a young girl from a devoutly religious home? A dope-head out of the inner city slums? A cruising butch lesbian on the prowl? Do you see eye to eye with a deserted mother working overtime to support three latch-key children? How about a trucker about to lose his rig? A man who grew up in a hippie commune in New Mexico? A woman who spent years of her youth with the Weatherman in the period when sexual fidelity was forbidden? A group of high-schoolers caught up in today's wave of satanism?

Thing is, if you fail to understand the thinking, attitudes, and feelings of people in other milieus within our culture, you limit yourself drastically in your choice of characters.

Case in point: An older writer of my acquaintance was in the process of working up a female character. He needed a contemporary romantic song as part of the atmosphere, so he consulted his nearest available expert on pop music, a young professional woman who lived next door.

"What," he asked, "is an appropriate number for a girl to be seduced by these days?"

A moment's pause, while Expert pondered. Then a giggle.

"More likely," she said, "she'll do the seducing." And then, after another giggle: "I mean, it's liberation time. These days, guys don't always take the lead."

She went on from there. By the time she got through, my friend, grinning wryly, admitted he'd learned all sorts of things.

Finally, Expert glanced at her watch. "Hey, I better go. Ed should have supper on by now."

It turned out that Ed, her live-in boyfriend, was cook for this particular contemporary family. He also did the laundry and ironed his own shirts. And neither he nor the young woman seemed to find anything unusual about the situation.

This didn't surprise me too much, but it certainly did my friend, because it contradicted major concepts he'd held since childhood. Being older, the fact that a whole broad range of traditional behavior patterns had reversed for many people simply hadn't dawned on him. Today's focus on instant gratification had passed him by.

He was unaware of how great a role conspicuous consumption plays with the present generation; how men and women coming out of school take it for granted that they can automatically step into the level of living their parents worked twenty or thirty years to attain; that one-on-one dating is pretty much out of style, replaced by small-group get-togethers. "Do your own thing" and "If it feels good, do it" were alien concepts to him. He didn't realize that what he thought of as irresponsibility was a state of mind that said self-expression and individuality were more important than staying with an unsatisfying job. Or that authority is no longer accepted for its own sake, and that a large segment of society takes affluence for granted.

The lesson here is, as my friend discovered, times have changed, so the things your characters think and do should reflect it.

Further, age is far from being the only issue. Whether you're seventeen or twenty-seven or thirty-seven, you're in contact every day with people who have different feelings and attitudes than you do, even if they don't express them.

These people aren't different just in occupation. Take, for example, men and women who have done their share of time in law enforcement. They have a different view of life than do civilians, see the people they meet through different eyes. Years of dealing with "perps," lawbreakers, tends to make them suspicious, cynical. To a degree they tend to live in a closed society of their kind.

These are facts you need to recognize if you hope to achieve any degree of realism when you use an officer as a character. He's not just a man; he is, in effect, a member of a special club. And while you may modify such elements to suit your needs and tastes, you don't dare to ignore it.

This is relatively close to the normal pattern. You can understand such people without too much difficulty and adjust your handling of them as characters to fit.

How about individuals further out, however: career criminals, pedophiles, Black Moslems, you name it? Each lives in his own closed world-within-the-world, separated from outsiders by unvoiced beliefs and attitudes and feelings. The young woman working in a massage parlor has a private view of her customers and it's unlikely to be the same as theirs. The outlook of the debutante — or her wealthy parents — may be one of disbelief at the pattern accepted as routine by the medical technician. The priest's words from the pulpit may not be at all the same as his private thoughts. And anyone who has made even casual contact with the "simple life" of the various Old Order Amish groups knows that in its way it can be ever so complex, with taboos and sanctions that may govern anything from dress to farming. Some fellowships restrict transportation to buggies; others permit cars if they're painted black—and that includes even the bumpers. There are bodies that feel marriage of a boy or girl even to a member of another Amish group is grounds for the form of ostracism termed "shunning."

Bear in mind that as the world changes, attitudes do too. Whose approach to casual sex can stay the same in a society where AIDS and its consequences hold the headlines? So-called "safe sex" has remolded the moonlight-and-roses of romance into a routine with clinical overtones.

Those are today's facts of life and we all know them—more or less, that is. But all too often they don't reach our fiction, the stories we tell. Instead, we write of a never-never land in which the characters are those from our childhood fantasies.

I have no objection to this, you understand, for I find fiction decked out in sociological terms less than a prize package. But failure to show awareness of the changing world creates both plot and character problems and, more often than not, destroys the realism of your story. Indeed, it's entirely possible that one of the reasons editors feel your work isn't on track is because it reflects beliefs, fears, and prejudices that don't ring true for the contemporary present you're striving to portray.

Nor do I mean that you've necessarily made your story world as out-of-date as the old pulp detective stories in which the villain escaped on a street car. Quite possibly the issue is merely a matter of obsolete slang or thinking or hairstyles, or reference to events meaningless to present-day readers. All such change rapidly; witness today's sudden surge of media attention on the environment, the homeless, and high medical costs.

How do you insure that your characters are reasonably in touch with their particular aspect of the contemporary world, that their ideas and fears and thinking are geared to their roles, yet not so tied to fads as to be outdated tomorrow?

1. Read.
A trick I've found useful is to select a specialized magazine or

two that reflects the world in which Character's going to be involved, whether *Rolling Stone* or *MAD* or *Easy Rider*. Reading between the lines, you may gain insight into elements ranging from topic preoccupation to pay scales, legal issues to injuries on the job.

Same for other enclaves. Are you dealing with people with more money than you'll ever see? Try *Town and Country, Connoisseur, Vanity Fair,* and *Architectural Digest. Family Circle, Woman's Day,* and *Better Homes and Gardens* tend to reflect the housewife's world. Employed and career women may shape and be shaped by *Working Woman, Executive Female, Women in Business,* and *New Woman.*

In the same way, read travel magazines for "in" places characters can visit and color details they can cite. Read fashion magazines, for what your characters wear and how they feel about it. Read sports magazines, so your people can sound half-way like normal human beings in incidental conversation. Read *Mademoiselle* and *Cosmopolitan* and *Glamour* to get an idea of what today's young women are interested in and think about; read *GQ* and *Playboy* for men. Read specialty magazines, so your characters can voice an infatuation with motorcycles or woodworking or the outdoors. Give them interests and opinions and let them talk about them.

Their reactions may be positive or negative. Just because a trend exists doesn't mean your character must go with it. It's perfectly legitimate for him to be on the other side — maybe outraged by it. Which can make for fine misunderstandings and conflicts between your story people to help you build your book or story.

(Again, a case in point: A girl I met spoke bitterly of how boys, despite her protests, always took her for pizza, a food she detested.)

Thing is, do your reading carefully. Check each and every fragment, whether copy or advertising, that surprises you or strikes you as new or out of key with your own view of life. Indeed, even your daily papers and news magazines can help, if you watch for the right fragments.

Example: The other day I chanced upon a feature about an organization called Debtors Anonymous, which attempted to salvage people trapped in the morass of credit card buying. The picture it drew, the trend it revealed, was one that provided a model contemporary touch for some character who buys and buys and buys until engulfed in debt, simply because credit is available and spending provides luxuries and flash that makes him feel important.

Further, even though the organization goes away, the problem won't, so you can use it.

Does all this reading mean spending a fortune on printed matter? No. Libraries have periodical rooms that overflow with all sorts of publications. Take advantage of them.

But don't expect reading to create characters for you. You need to back it up with personal contact with all sorts of people wherever possible, so some nuance you haven't captured won't end up making one of your story people — and you — look ridiculous.

2. Listen.

Sounds do make a difference. The network TV shows will give you a picture of the world otherwise unavailable. Talk show radio is particularly valuable. So is junk television, with its continual deluge of interviews by Phil Donahue, Oprah Winfrey, Geraldo Rivera, and all the rest. New pop music and MTV help to capture the spirit of our period.

Catch people talking. Become an eavesdropper. And not just on your friends. Try to hear what people outside your normal range of contacts have to say about abortion, corruption, homelessness, crime, the new buses, the old beggars, everything. The slurs, the stumbles, the mumbles, the nasals, the shrill jangles, the repetitions. Look always for the slang, the cant, the distortions and deviations.

3. Look.

At how people behave, that is. Go to restaurants. Cruise the thrift shops. Spend time in bars, parks, campuses, shopping malls, courtrooms.

Check out the new styles, in store windows and on warm bodies of all ages. The old styles, too. The people who swarm about you — fat, thin, erect, slouched, stylish, sophisticated, dowdy, dirty. Give an eye to their hair — home cut, salon styled, GI cropped. How many rings do they wear? On what fingers? How about earrings, single or multiple?

Above all — and this takes in everything that's been said above — be aware. Given awareness, you'll find you can work through every problem.

Including the biggest problem of all, that of disbelief, the refusal of readers to accept your story. There are techniques to meet that, too. We'll discuss them in Chapter 16.

16

THE DYNAMICS OF DISBELIEF

How do you cope when readers don't believe in your characters and stories? You plug the gaps where belief leaks out.

I t's a fine story, the best you've ever written. Yet all it garners when you submit it is rejection. Why? Because, the editors say, there's something wrong with one or more of the characters. Somehow, they ring false. Readers just can't believe them.

Whatever that means.

Well, what *does* it mean?

Bedrock, first. Fiction, it has been said, is based on a willing suspension of disbelief.

That is, readers know a story isn't real, isn't true. But in their role of fiction fans, on an unconscious level they pretend it *is* true, accept it and live through it with the characters.

A. Conan Doyle's classic science fiction adventure novel, *The Lost World,* is a good example. It offers an imaginary world high on an unexplored South American plateau inhabited by a variety of prehistoric monsters.

Intellectually, most readers know such a "lost world" doesn't really exist. But the concept fascinates them, so they read on, caught up in the excitement that engulfs Professor Challenger and his companions. During the time they spend with the book, they suspend their disbelief, their knowledge that the situation and the story aren't true.

The same principle applies to today's top fiction figures, from Perry Mason to Gideon Oliver, Louis L'Amour's western heroes and Fred Pohl's science creations, even film and TV people like Rambo, Freddie (of *Nightmare on Elm Street* fame), Jessica Fletcher, and Murphy Brown.

Your story, in contrast, simply didn't bring that acceptance of the imaginary, that suspension of disbelief. Allegedly, it's because of some flaw or flaws in your presentation of the characters.

What flaws? What are some of the things your characters can do that disrupt readers' suspension of disbelief in regard to your story?

You name it. The number of possibilities is virtually endless. But the bulk fall into seven major categories.

Specifically:

1. You can fall out of viewpoint.
2. You can fail to do enough research.
3. You can tell your story instead of showing it.
4. You can leave gaps in the motivation/reaction (M/R) stairway.
5. You can fail to plant the things you should.
6. You can give your characters things to do that your readers find distasteful.
7. You can make the characters themselves less than likable.

Let's take these one at a time.

1. Viewpoint weaknesses

Viewpoint, as I've said at some length elsewhere, is the angle or position from which you present your story. Ordinarily, that involves a "Whose skin are you in?" approach, a selection of a person who tells the story or through whose experiences it's seen/heard/smelled/tasted/touched/thought/felt.

Viewpoint goes far beyond the physical, however. It isn't just the point or person we're seeing the story from; it's *how* we're seeing, and the essence of that *how* lies in the viewpoint character's beliefs and attitudes and prejudices, the emotion that drives him, the way he *reacts* to what happens, the stimuli that impinge on him.

Each of us responds to each person we meet, each thing that happens, according to our already existing attitudes, our feelings. If I feel my brother is forever bossing me, I may respond with hostility instead of gratitude when he, with the best possible intentions, lines me up for a high-pay job. As an aging mother, I may burst into tears of grief if my daughter—again, with all good intentions—surprises me with the gift of a luxury condo that will take me away from my run-down neighborhood, with its familiar church and stores and all my friends. And I still remember a fist-fight I had under a small-town street light because I'd unknowingly outraged another boy by calling him by a middle name he hated.

Is this matter of emotion and experience conditioned reactions limited just to stimuli from people? No, of course not. We respond to everything in the world about us, from weather to decor to what's on our plate at dinner. Automatically and without volition, we act out our feelings and past conditionings on everyone and everything we experience . . . pass judgment on events and circumstances as well as individuals. Thus, a man or woman registers on us when we meet him or her: "What a slut!" "How dowdy!" "What an oaf!" "Too slick to trust," "Oh, God, another women's libber!" "Those hands! Arthritis that bad, how can he hold a steering wheel? They ought to take away his license."

But we also have other feelings: "Damn lawn! I hate it." "Rain, rain, rain. I've got to find a better climate." "When will I get bright and lay off the beer?"

Such attitudes, insofar as they bear on your story, need to be taken into account as you conceive, develop, and write about your viewpoint character.

Does this mean we must continually bounce in and out of your viewpoint character's mind?

No, of course not. The key issue is that you've thought Character through to the point that you write about him *as if* his attitudes were on parade, even though we never state them. We reveal them in such fragments as "He eyed her quizzically," as contrasted with "Coldly, she looked him up and down"; "She touched his arm. 'Here, let me help you' " instead of " 'Move over, Jack. I'll handle that.' "

Is this important? Yes. When your story's properly in viewpoint, inside somebody's head, your reader well-nigh automatically identifies with that somebody.

Beyond this, viewpoint flaws lead to disbelief when they *confuse* your reader . . . when they show a character who doesn't ring true to reader . . . that goes against your reader's own experience with life and people. Then the reader is shunted off the smooth flow of the story. In spite of himself, he frowns. Logical thinking and questioning, replaces the hypnotic state the story's induced and, too often, disbelief moves in to replace it.

If you jump about in viewpoint, entering one skin, one head, after another, your reader's likely to have difficulty following the story's emotional line, for automatically, the change jolts him. It's as if you were lining up a final putt in a golf game, your every iota of attention focused on it. Then, some idiot behind you says, "Hey, look at his frayed sweater," or "That's sure not the way I'd play that." It's not surprising, under such circumstances, that you'll miss the shot—and neither is it surprising if, in a story, a viewpoint change will distract a reader.

It's even worse when viewpoint is, for the moment, unclear, and readers don't know whose skin they're in. Do avoid it!

I'm not talking about major viewpoint changes, you understand, as when you're moving from one chapter to another. There, you're going to stay with one of your story people long enough that the confusion issue is minimized. But even then it's highly desirable to establish time, place, circumstance, and viewpoint whenever a change in any of them are made. Do it as soon as possible, as in terms of on Page One; even better, in Paragraph One or Two.

There are two other points I'm going to put under this category of viewpoint flaws, even though some might question their inclusion.

First, readers seldom like a stupid character as viewpoint. To take an all-too-common example, the heroine in a mystery or romance receives a message telling her to go alone to the blood-drenched tower of the old manse at midnight for whatever reason. Heroine goes—and Reader throws down the book in disgust because he can't believe that any modern woman in her right mind would so act. By failing to show even reasonable common sense, Heroine has lost his sympathy and shattered his acceptance of the story. He no longer wants to identify with Heroine, because none of us care to feel stupid—which Heroine, behaving in a stupid manner, now makes us feel. Where Reader's concerned, Heroine and story no longer are believable.

Same way, Hero, weaponless, charges in on three armed killers, apparently operating on the "My strength is as the strength of ten because my heart is pure" theory. Well, maybe. But readers will accept the clash more easily if Hero also has at least a vestige of an intelligent plan, even though in execution said plan fails and he has to wing it.

It's hard, too, to think of Villain as a real menace if he has Hero trapped and all he has to do is pull the trigger to solve all problems, only instead he launches into a long-winded explanation of why he's going to postpone Hero's demise till a later time or place, meanwhile leaving Hero tied up and thus given an opportunity to escape.

Enough of stupidity. Let's move on to point two, the negative aspects of intelligence.

Too great intelligence *is* negative where a viewpoint character is concerned. The acceptable hero or heroine will prove more satisfactory if he or she is a solid normal, for most of us are less than enthusiastic about the individual we think of as The Brain. Why? Because we know we ourselves aren't all that smart, and we feel uncomfortable with or inferior to the person who clearly is our superior.

If you do want a brilliant hero or heroine, make him or her modest too. Or present him as Rex Stout handled Nero Wolfe: brilliant but with foibles, and with an ever-so-down-to-earth normal aide, Archie Goodwin, as viewpoint.

Finally, remember that the things a character notices and the amount of space you, the author, devote to that noticing are part of characterization.

Take these lines from Earl Emerson's *Fat Tuesday.* We're in the hero's viewpoint as he interviews a mother. Three children come in, and there's a bit of byplay establishing them. Then the mother says,

> *"There's a stain on your dress, young lady." The girl peered down guiltily.*
> *"Michelle did it."*
> *"Lucy." Veronica Rogers's tone was controlled, but the message stung. Lucy turned around obediently and marched away behind the two boys. She didn't need spurs for these kids. Like a Comanche warrior on horseback, she had them trained to knee commands.*

You see? Mother acts, and her action characterizes her. Hero notices and interprets, *in character,* and that characterizes him.

Or here, when Hero gives his first major description of the mother:

Mrs. Rogers had short blond hair and a tan that, considering the Northwest's winters, had probably been nursed under a sunlamp. She was one of those women who made you wonder how far the tan extended. You felt impolite wondering, but you wondered all the same. She wore a loose print blouse under a waist-length jacket and expensively faded charcoal jeans that were tight enough to make you remember them but not so tight as to beg fashion. Her high-heeled shoes were a bright cherry red, her sockless feet evenly brown.

Clearly, the amount of space, of description, of this woman not only draws a picture of her but indicates that she's important to the story. And the *manner* in which Author has Hero describe her, the details picked out for emphasis, show us the state of mind, the feelings, she engenders in Hero. Despite her cool, controlled appearance, Hero's interested in her—to a degree sexually interested—but not panting; and the ground is laid for further developments and the climax of the book. It's a skilled use of viewpoint by Emerson.

2. Inadequate research

Here we're talking about things important to the story that Writer should know. Why? Because if he doesn't, readers quite possibly will. Author's failure to know them automatically raises the thought in Reader's mind, "This guy doesn't know what he's talking about—so why should I bother to read him?" Again, belief has been shattered. When you don't know the difference between a rifle and shotgun, or organdy and tulle, it's a mark against you.

We've already talked about the business of research in terms of the technical, not-so-trivial trivia writers too often slight—the revolvers with safeties, etchings versus woodcuts, the nature of a geode. But failure to do adequate research goes beyond that, and I do mean into the realm of character.

This most often involves matters of attitude. Too often, we assume that all people—and all characters—feel and think as we do, and that simply isn't so.

For example, how is a frontier mother supposed to feel about hostile Indians? A contemporary business man about unions? A retiree with three small rental houses about subsidized housing?

What turn of mind led young girls to become Charles Manson groupies or biker mamas?

The key to answering all these questions is, of course, research. Is it worth while? Yes. The perfect example is a fragment in Mark Twain's *Huckleberry Finn*. Huck has disguised himself as a girl. But a woman penetrates the ruse instantly because Huck clamps his legs together when she tosses him a lump of lead to throw at a rat. A girl wouldn't have done so, because a lifetime of wearing skirts would have conditioned her to spread her knees to catch a thrown object.

How did Twain find the basis for this bit? Obviously, he did research—kept his eyes open for incidents he could use in his writing.

3. Telling

Versus showing, that is.

Showing brings belief. Telling doesn't.

At least, not necessarily.

Take the case of the woman who says to you, in regard to a neighbor, "She's no better than she should be." Perhaps she elaborates with stories of Neighbor's sexual misconduct.

Do you believe her? Maybe. Or maybe not.

On the other hand, you're walking through the park tonight and take a short-cut. Off to one side, partially concealed in a clump of bushes, lies the woman you've been told about. She's locked in a steamy embrace with a man.

Do you believe your eyes, what you yourself are seeing?

Yes. You simply can't deny that kind of visual evidence.

The same principle applies when I claim I can levitate myself—rise from my chair and move through the air this way and that. If I tell you about it, you may nod politely, but you're hardly likely to believe me. But if I demonstrate by actually performing the feat, you're forced to accept the truth of my statement.

Same for opening a vault a la Jimmy Valentine, "feeling" the combination with my super-sensitive fingers. Or reading someone's mind by pure power of will. Or talking up my derring-do as a soldier or scholar or explorer versus having a diploma or display of medals hanging on the wall, or showing you a scrapbook full of clips of my exploits.

Do learn to write your stories in terms of such proof. *Show* things happening; don't just *tell* about them.

4. M/R gaps

A story is made up of a succession of scenes and sequels, units of confrontation/conflict and units of transition/decision. In general, action and development within a scene is continuous. It consists of a series of motivations and reactions (M/R): first a stimulus from outside the viewpoint character, then the viewpoint character's response — in character — to that stimulus . . . which brings on another motivating stimulus from the person or circumstance being confronted . . . which calls forth another reaction . . . and so on, as when someone speaks to you; you answer; the other person responds to your answer; which leads to you speaking again, making yet another remark . . . until the scene, the confrontation, is ended. (I'm oversimplifying here. For a more detailed development, see my *Techniques of the Selling Writer.*)

Thing is, a scene, a unit of conflict, is made up of a continuous series of these stimulus/response or motivation/reaction units. It's what gives your readers the feeling they're living through the experience.

If you don't follow this pattern of development, however, if you allow spots to creep in where a motivation doesn't lead to a reaction, or a reaction flashes on sans motivation, you jar your reader, gamble with his suspension of disbelief.

I call these breaks, these holes where motivation isn't linked to reaction, gaps in the M/R stairway, because a scene's development very well may be compared with a flight of steps — each motivation a riser, each reaction a tread. Leave out either a riser or a tread and Reader is likely to stumble or fall where his sense of continuity and building tension are concerned.

Let your reader be thrown off balance too many times, and she may decide that something's wrong with your story, even though she can't say what.

Thus, if Hero slaps Heroine and she gives no indication of it, or if a character touches a hot stove but doesn't respond by jerking back, your story people aren't behaving realistically. Increasingly, readers have difficulty believing them.

In sequels, units of transition and decision between scenes, action isn't necessarily continuous. A character may wander around for hours or days, take care of incidental business while brooding about a problem and trying to decide what to do. But in scenes, the units of confrontation/conflict where action is continuous, gaps in the M/R stairway can really shatter a story. Watch out for them.

5. Planting

We've talked about planting before. But since the lack of it can be a major cause of reader disbelief, it warrants a bit further attention here.

To *plant* something means to stick that something into your story early in the game because you know you're going to need it later. Case in point: Hero is going to need a gun with which to shoot Villain or hold him at bay. So, you *plant* a gun—that is, reveal its presence to your readers—in a desk drawer within the first few pages and let someone on your hero's side—the heroine, perhaps—be aware of it. You don't make an issue of it, you understand; you simply make it obvious that it's there.

Now, story nears climax. Villain holds Hero at bay with some lethal weapon. Heroine stands off to one side, next to the desk, well-nigh petrified with fear. Hero charges Villain and is appropriately clobbered. Villain raises his weapon to finish groggy hero off. Whereupon, the realization that Hero's about to die shatters Heroine's paralysis. She claws open the drawer that holds the gun and fires at Villain. Because she lacks experience with firearms, she misses. But the crash of the gunshot distracts Villain momentarily. In that moment, Hero regains his feet and knocks Villain cold. Clinch and close.

(Why does Heroine miss? Because in the past, reader anticipation ordinarily demanded that Hero should, by his own valor, triumph. Heroine was expected to be gentle, passive, hapless, and hopeless. Is this a sexist handling? Yes. In many of today's stories, Heroine would be a crack shot, drop Villain in his tracks, and be the final victor. You plan your climax to fit your market.)

Must all planting be so obvious? No. You can be as crude or subtle as your story and your editor permit.

Further, planting is by no means limited to objects. You can—and should—also plant *character traits,* as in the example from *Fat Tuesday,* above. A character who kicks dogs and pulls the wings off flies seldom proves to be the hero. And when Heroine spends the money she's saved for a wedding dress to buy an air conditioner or smoke detector for the impoverished old lady next door, readers will tend to think well of her.

Abilities, too, need to be planted. If someone must ferret out what's wrong with a broken-down pickup, establish him as a mechanically minded car buff earlier. Training as a nurse sets up a woman to take over at the scene of an accident. A hairdresser is likely to be able to detect dyed tresses. An accountant will look at doctored books with more insight than will a layman.

Closely related to this is the ability of a character to note significant details, and the key word here is "significant." Take a priest who, despite vows of poverty, drives a flashy sports car. This is significant only if it indicates an aspect of the priest's character or is a plant to explain his contacts or such. It is not significant if he only drives it temporarily because it was donated and he can't sell it for the cost of a plain four-door sedan. Same for a skeleton hanging on a rack in Heroine's bedroom or her mother's fondness for a patent medicine that contains 40 percent alcohol. If these details don't contribute to the plot they're not significant and shouldn't be mentioned.

Note, too, that *plant* to a large degree means *show*. It's hard to plant something that can't be seen or heard or whatever. (In print fiction you certainly may plant an odor, for instance, or a taste. Since you're in a character's head, you may report anything Character experiences.)

When you plant something, however, bear in mind that you're obligated to *pay off* said plant. If you make a thing of the gun in the drawer, readers will expect someone to use it later. Same for love letters, emerald necklaces, the fragrance of roses, or a bad disposition.

6. Distaste/denial

How much realism is acceptable in a story where your characters' behavior is concerned? And will too much tend to aggravate readers sufficiently as to shatter their suspension of disbelief? It's something to consider.

In a book I read recently, a character was shown helping to put an elderly invalid "on the pot." I found it integral to the story and totally inoffensive. An acquaintance, however, did not. "Disgusting" and "revolting" were the mildest terms she used to describe the bit, and I wondered what dimension her vocabulary would

reach were she to read some of the passages in Thomas Harris's
The Silence of the Lambs.

In the same way, some readers may be bothered by a scene in
which a diabetic character takes an insulin shot. If you include rape
or attack details in a story, you take a chance. Bloody descriptions
of accidents or surgery or war are *verboten* to some readers. Same
for death and desolation. Howard Fast's description of the final
fate of his subject's bones in the biographical novel *Citizen Tom
Paine* haunted me for months. (The bones were lost forever in England when a mountebank couldn't get a permit to exhibit them
for pay.)

This problem isn't limited to the written word. Toulouse-Lau-
trec's painting that depicts two whores waiting in line for medical
inspection is distressing to many viewers. Hogarth's engravings of
The Rake's Progress still draw adverse reactions.

The issue is, of course, the audience. Judy Blume was con-
demned because her writings for young people dealt realistically
with situations — divorce and family and adolescent problems — that
disturbed adults. Though S. E. Hinton won awards with books like
The Outsiders, whose characters are slum Chicano adolescents,
many parents felt they had no place on their children's school reading lists. The people in romance novels, horror stories, and mysteries upset many readers to the point that they reject all such. And
Frederic Wertham received national publicity for his outrage at the
gorier comic books, in one of which characters used a severed head
as a baseball.

This in no way means that I'm suggesting you self-censor your
work. But you should at least be aware that some characters and
actions can be distasteful to some readers. These individuals show
their displeasure by walking wide around or refusing to read your
epics, as is their right. So consider it a possible factor where disbelief
is concerned.

7. Non-likable characters

Readers and editors can reject — refuse to believe — your story
if they don't find at least one of your characters likable.

To put it another way, readers and editors are strong for stories
with a positive emotional orientation.

Such an orientation means that, in the old Hollywood phrase,
readers have "someone to cheer for."

"Who do we cheer for?" really means, "What character do we want to see win?"

The character readers want to see win has three basic traits.

1. The character is striving to attain something.

That is, he or she is goal-oriented, purpose-oriented. So, in striving, the character can win or lose. This gives you, in story terms, suspense.

2. The character is today-slanted.

That is, he fits in with current reality as your readers know it.

We've already talked about the importance of zeroing in on the standards and behavior patterns of your readers. Here I'll only add that it can be difficult to keep on top of things in a society whose mores and standards are continually in a state of flux. Mass audiences today may not accept a woman who sacrifices a blossoming career in order to stroke her husband's ego by staying home and canning food "just like Mother used to make"—because that's not society as they know it. And I doubt that a pro-drug epic like *Easy Rider* would find financial backing today. In a phrase, times have changed.

3. The character does not contradict readers' feelings or their basic beliefs.

In other words, despite all changes, the right and wrong issue remains important. Most readers, most of the time, prefer to stand on the side of the angels rather than of Satan. It's difficult for them to cheer for someone who outrages their sense of what's good and what's bad, or whose behavior and beliefs are on a different track from theirs.

Thus, by and large, it upsets most readers to be asked to cheer for—that is, identify positively with—rapists or serial killers, or abusive husbands or spendthrift wives or belligerently nasty children.

This means that ordinarily the character they *do* cheer for, male or female, will be one who thinks and acts in a manner that reflects the standards and mores of that group of readers for whom your work is destined.

Not that this is likely to be easy to determine in a society as complex and ever-shifting as ours. Nor will the character you develop necessarily be admirable or even likable in the accepted sense. But he *will* be a person readers can understand and empathize with in his striving, and he'll fit into the world they know, and in the final clutch at least he'll stand for the right thing as he sees it . . . show the "climax potential" we talked about in Chapter 10.

Which will make him a likable character indeed in the broadest, most meaningful sense. I urge you to search him out and build him. Believe me, it will pay off.

So much for at least seven of the reasons why readers may fail to believe your stories. But be that as it may, and whatever the incidental hazards, a writer by his nature wants to write. That makes characters ever so much his business—and his salvation. We'll talk about it in our final chapter, "The Search for Zest."

17

THE SEARCH FOR ZEST

*How do you maintain your cutting
edge as a writer?
You draw on the stimulus of
story people.*

A friend who's a highly successful author of historical novels tells me that the actual writing of his books leaves him cold. What locks him to the craft is that it gives him an excuse to do research—to explore new areas of knowledge for intriguing facts and twists.

I suggest that you apply a variation of the same principle to your work in building characters. That is, that you scan and explore and analyze people every chance you get. Where you used simply to dismiss some people as not worth getting to know, now you observe and probe and try to understand. Instead of avoiding an obnoxious man or woman, ask yourself, "What makes a person act this way?" Look for details—how a person continually rubs fingers together, bares teeth, tries to glower into your eyes, whatever. Every encounter is grist for your character mill if you see it as, one way or another, fascinating.

Why? Because character study very probably is your best way to escape the fatigue and boredom that endless hours of writing often bring.

Thing is, there's an infinity of people to draw on for your stories. Each one is different. Don't hesitate to study them. Take it upon yourself to find something fresh and new in each and every person. Rationalize to the farthest limits of your imagination.

Believe me, the process will excite you. And out of that excitement will come production.

People read fiction for feeling. Whether they know it or not, they grope for stimuli that move them.

The thing in fiction that gives them this stimulation is emotion projected through characters — story people.

Characters become readers' friends. Looking back over the infinity of memorable stories I've read, I can remember the people, but seldom the adventures. Sherlock Holmes and Travis McGee both have stayed with me. So have Tom Sawyer, Huck Finn, Rhett Butler and Scarlett O'Hara, Sam Spade, Moll Flanders and Fanny Hill, D'Artagnan and Oliver Twist, Ivanhoe, Fagan, Shylock, Destry, Shane, Blind Pew, Long John Silver, Perry Mason, Tarzan, and Don Camillo.

For you as a writer, concentrating on routine cardboard characters is the kiss of death. Why? Because you get tired of stereotyped story people, people with reactions so predictable that they put you to sleep before you even set them down.

You can't afford that. The secret to avoiding it is to deal with each member of your cast as a unique and special individual who intrigues you. Only thus can you maintain your own interest and enthusiasm.

This is true even when you're writing of series characters, so common in the mystery field. There you may grow weary of the continuing protagonist, so you gain your zest from the subsidiary figures introduced in each new story. These people are individual and unique. They have new, fresh problems. The central character, the continuing protagonist with whom you're bored, in effect serves as a hired gun who fights the others' battles for them. While we thrill to the way he handles it, the new individual, the new threat or puzzle, provides a focus for our interest.

(To see this technique handled by a master, read back over any of John D. MacDonald's Travis McGee stories.)

How have I come to all these conclusions about maintaining interest? Well, back in the '50s, I was assigned to script two films on boredom for a mental health group. It was an enlightening experience. In essence, boredom, I discovered (though it's hardly a tremendous or unique insight), is a conflict state, in which duty, conditioning, or some other element demands you do one thing, when consciously or otherwise, you want to be doing something else.

Apply this to your situation as a writer. In essence, when you grow bored, you're tired of whatever it is you're writing. You'd much rather be partying or fishing or playing poker or lolling on the beach. But conscience or economic necessity say you should be hammering out words.

But why are you bored? The answer is that your story no longer stimulates you, excites you.

Why doesn't it stimulate you?

There can be all sorts of reasons. But one of the most common is that you've drawn too much from the well without refilling.

The well, of course, is your own head. Your brain. Your consciousness. Your imagination. You've drained it of things that interest and intrigue you.

Or, to put it another way, you've used the same story elements too often: the same ideas, the same settings, the same twists and complications, the same characters.

Especially the same characters.

Has this necessarily been a conscious process? No, of course not. It's just that, reaching out for the next phrase, the next sentence, the next development, your tired gray cells (to steal a term from Agatha Christie's famed Hercule Poirot) came up with familiar fragments, bits and pieces you'd used or at least mulled over before.

That brought little excitement to you or your copy, any more than scrubbing the floor for the thousandth time turns on a housewife. The difference is that scrubbing or dishwashing is mechanical. It doesn't demand new, fresh patterns or procedures.

Writing's something else again. After awhile and a hundred or a thousand reworkings of essentially the same pattern, you found your mind wandering and, quite possibly without even being aware of it, you wished you were doing something else.

Indeed, were I to face you in person at that moment and accuse you of such feelings, you might very well be outraged. "That's just not true!" you very well might protest. "I'm working, working hard. But the words just won't come right."

So far as your own awareness was concerned, you'd be right. But your enthusiasm would still be gone.

How, then, do you maintain your enthusiasm, your zest for work?

The answer is, refill the well! Search out new experiences. Give the mind-pool that is your imagination, your subconscious, a chance to accumulate new stimuli.

That means, work with more and different raw material — fresh settings, fresh plot concepts, fresh story people.

Especially fresh story people.

The reason for this is that plots and settings are by their very nature more or less limited. (Remember George Polti's *The Thirty-Six Dramatic Situations?* Other analysts claim to have stripped the total down to three, or four, or a dozen.) But characters are not. Infinite in variety, beyond measurement in numbers, they strike sparks in your imagination without conscious effort on your part. For example:

- the young woman, tired of mowing her lawn, who outraged her neighbors by replacing grass with gravel.
- the old man who had his tombstone carved with a date of death while he was still alive.
- the attorney who infuriated a judge by wearing a turban and see-through shirt in court.

These are only springboards, of course—jumping-off places from which a character or story may develop. You have dozens more as enlivening in your own head. But explored more deeply, amplified in terms of a thousand "what ifs" and permutations, it's just possible that they or others like them will excite you—rouse you to enthusiasm, or even zest.

What is zest?

"Hearty enjoyment," the dictionary says. "Gusto."

In your case, a sudden, surging desire to make something out of nothing.

A story.

If you can capture that feeling, that pulsing excitement of snaring and twisting and molding and expanding new ideas, you'll never stop writing. Though you may slow down or, like Somerset Maugham in his last years, officially retire, the pictures of unique people in tension-creating situations will still rouse you, the way they say the firebell used to rouse the old firehorse.

Listen to Martha Kay Renfroe, mystery author, referring to one of her series characters: ". . . I like Conan [Flagg]. I plan to stick with him for a long time to come."

With that cornerstone around which to build your life, what more can any writer want?

To all of you, then, may each character you create prove a new thrill. And may those story people delight you and your readers!

APPENDIX: FOR FURTHER READING

Let's face it, I'm a book freak. Consequently, the temptation to load you down with an endless bibliography is strong upon me, but I'm going to do my best to hold it within reasonable bounds.

With a few exceptions, the works included in this list deal with either (a.) writing or (b.) human psychology or sociology. In most instances, they're down to earth. They offer practical information and ideas which, with luck, you may be able actually to apply to your own work.

One word of warning: Please don't let poking around in these books or any others come to serve as a substitute for putting words of your own on paper. A writer's job, ever and always, is to write, remember, so the basic issue is—Write On!

Adler, Alfred. *Understanding Other People.* Cleveland: The World Publishing Co., 1941.

Aronson, Eliot. *The Social Animal.* 5th ed. San Francisco: W.H. Freeman & Co., 1988.

Bedford-Jones, H. *This Fiction Business.* New York: Covici-Friede, 1929.

——. *The Graduate Fictioneer.* Denver: Author & Journalist Publishing Co., 1932.

Bickham, Jack M. *Writing Novels That Sell.* New York: Simon & Schuster, 1989.

Blinder, Martin. *Lovers, Killers, Husbands and Wives.* New York: St. Martin's Press, 1985.

Campbell, Walter S. *Writing Magazine Fiction.* Chapter 2, "Characterization." New York: Doubleday, Doran & Co., 1940.

Card, Orson Scott. *Characters & Viewpoint.* Cincinnati: Writer's Digest Books, 1988.

Cleckley, Hervey. *The Mask of Sanity.* New York: New American Library, 1982.

Cohen, Betsy. *The Snow White Syndrome.* New York: Macmillan Publishing Co., 1986.

Davis, Flora. *Inside Intuition: What We Know about Nonverbal Communication.* New York: McGraw-Hill Book Co., 1972.

Egri, Lajos. *The Art of Creative Writing.* New York: The Citadel Press, 1965.

Glasser, William. *The Identity Society.* New York: Harper & Row (Colophon Books), 1975.

Goldberg, Herb. *The New Male-Female Relationship.* New York: New American Library, 1984.

Harral, Stewart. *Keys to Successful Interviewing.* Chapter 3, "Are People Predictable?" Norman: University of Oklahoma Press, 1954.

Harris, Foster. *The Basic Formulas of Fiction.* Norman: University of Oklahoma Press, 1944.

Henslin, James M. *Down to Earth Sociology.* New York: The Free Press, 1981.

Hite, Shere. *The Hite Report on Female Sexuality*. New York: Macmillan, 1976.

— —. *The Hite Report on Male Sexuality*. New York: Alfred A. Knopf, 1981.

Keesing, Felix M. *Cultural Anthropology*. New York: Rinehart & Co., Inc., 1958.

Kerr, Walter. *How Not to Write a Play*. New York: Simon & Schuster, 1955.

Lasswell, Marcia, and Norman M. Lobsenz. *Styles of Loving*. New York: Doubleday & Co., 1980.

Macgowan, Kenneth. *A Primer of Playwriting*. New York: Doubleday & Co. (Dolphin Books), 1962.

McGaw, Charles. *Acting Is Believing*. New York: Holt, Rinehart & Winston, 1980.

McHugh, Vincent. *Primer of the Novel*. New York: Random House, 1950.

Melville, Keith. *Marriage and Family Today*. New York: Random House, 1977.

Monte, Christopher F. *Beneath the Mask: An Introduction to Theories of Personality*. New York: Praeger Publisher, 1977.

Mystery Writers of America. *Mystery Writer's Handbook*. Cincinnati: Writer's Digest, 1976.

Noyes, Arther P. *Modern Clinical Psychiatry*. 4th ed. Chapter 4, "Mental Mechanisms and Their Functions." Philadelphia: W.B. Saunders Co., 1953.

Palmer, Stuart. *Understanding Other People*. New York: Thomas Y. Crowell Co., 1955.

Peck, Robert Newton. *Fiction Is Folks*. Cincinnati: Writer's Digest Books, 1983.

Putney, Snell and Gail. *The Adjusted American*. New York: Harper & Row (Colophon Books), 1966.

Ray, Marie Benon. *The Importance of Feeling Inferior*. New York: Ace Books, 1957.

Sheehy, Gail. *Passages*. New York: Bantam Books, 1977.

Sicard, Gerald L. and Philip Weinberger. *Sociology for Our Times*. Glenview: Scott, Foresman & Co., 1977.

Swain, Dwight V. *Techniques of the Selling Writer*. Norman: University of Oklahoma Press, 1974.

Terkel, Studs. *Working*. New York: Avon Books, 1975.

Walters, Barbara. *How to Talk with Practically Anybody about Practically Anything*. New York: Dell Publishing Co., 1970.

Whetmore, Edward Jay. *Mediamerica*. Belmont, California: Wadsworth Publishing Co., 1982.

Whitney, Phyllis A. *Guide to Fiction Writing*. Boston: The Writer; Inc., 1982.

Whyte, William H. *The Social Life of Small Urban Spaces*. Washington, D.C.: The Conservation Foundation, 1980.

Wolfe, Linda. *The Cosmo Report*. New York: Arbor House, 1981.

INDEX

More Great Books for Writers

Ten Steps to Publishing Children's Books—Get published in the popular genre of children's books! You'll discover vital tips from successful writers and illustrators to help you polish the skills necessary to make your dream come true. Plus, the input of editors offers a unique perspective from the publishing side of the industry. *#10534/ $24.95/128 pages/150 illus.*

2000 Children's Writer's & Illustrator's Market—This directory brings together the two key aspects of children's publishing—writing and illustrating. In one handy volume you'll find helpful articles on how to make it in this lucrative field, followed by 800 detailed listings of book publishers, magazines, audiovisual, audiotape and scriptwriting markets. *#10626/$21.99/400 pages*

Children's Writer's Word Book—Even the most original children's story won't get published if its language usage or sentence structure doesn't speak to young readers. You'll avoid these pitfalls with this fast-reference guide full of word lists, reading levels for synonyms and more! *#10649/$16.99/352 pages/paperback*

Writing and Illustrating Children's Books for Publication: Two Perspectives—Discover how to create a good, publishable manuscript in only eight weeks! You'll cover the writing process in its entirety—from generating ideas and getting started, to submitting a manuscript. Imaginative writing and illustrating exercises build on these lessons and provide fuel for your creative fires! *#10448/$24.95/128 pages/200 b&w illus., 16 page color insert*

How To Write and Illustrate Children's Books and Get Them Published—Find everything you need to know about breaking into the lucrative children's market. You'll discover how to write a sure-fire seller, how to create fresh and captivating illustrations, how to get your manuscript into the right buyer's hands and more! *#30082/$24.99/144 pages*

Writing for Children and Teenagers, 3rd Edition—Now in its third edition, this comprehensive guide gives you the up-to-date information you need to get published in the ever-expanding field of children's writing. *#10101/$14.99/272 pages/paperback*

Grammatically Correct: The Writer's Guide to Punctuation, Spelling, Style, Usage and Grammar—Write prose that's clear, concise and graceful! This comprehensive desk reference covers the nuts-and-bolts basics of punctuation, spelling and grammar, as well as essential tips and techniques for developing a smooth, inviting writing style. *#10529/$19.99/352 pages*

The Writer's Digest Dictionary of Concise Writing—Make your work leaner, crisper and clearer! Under the guidance of professional editor Robert Hartwell Fiske, you'll learn how to rid your work of common say-nothing phrases while making it tighter and easier to read and understand. *#10482/$19.99/352 pages*

The Children's Writer's Reference—What types of animals work best in picture books? What periods in history are most popular with kids? This guide gives children's writers all the answers they need to write and illustrate stories kids will love and publishers will buy. From pre-reader to young adult, children's writers of any age group and genre will find the special market information they need here. *#10604/$16.99/272 pages/ paperback*

How to Write Attention-Grabbing Query & Cover Letters—Use the secrets John Wood reveals to write queries perfectly tailored, too good to turn down! In this guidebook, you will discover why boldness beats blandness in queries everytime, ten basics you must have in your article queries, ten query blunders that can destroy publication chances and much more. *#10462/$17.99/208 pages*

The Writer's Digest Sourcebook for Building Believable Characters—Create unforgettable characters as you "attend" a roundtable where six novelists reveal their approaches to characterization. You'll probe your characters' backgrounds, beliefs and desires with a fill-in-the-blanks questionnaire. And a thesaurus of characteristics will help you develop the many other features no character should be without. *#10463/$17.99/ 288 pages*

The Writer's Digest Character Naming Sourcebook—Finally, you'll discover how to choose the perfect name to reflect your character's personality, ethnicity and place in history. Here you'll find 20,000 first and last names (and their meanings) from around the world! *#10390/$18.99/352 pages*

Writer's Encyclopedia, 3rd Edition—Rediscover this popular writer's reference—now with information about electronic resources, plus more than 100 new entries. You'll find facts, figures, definitions and examples designed to answer questions about every discipline connected with writing and to help you convey a professional image. *#10464/ $22.99/560 pages/62 b&w illus.*

How to Write and Sell Children's Picture Books—Learn how to put your picture book on paper and get it published—whether you're retelling a wonderful old tale, or spinning a splendid new yarn. *#10410/$17.99/192 pages*

The Writer's Digest Guide to Manuscript Formats—No matter how good your ideas, an unprofessional format will land your manuscript on the slush pile! You need this easy-to-follow guide on manuscript preparation and presentation—for everything from books and articles, to poems and plays. *#10025/$19.99/200 pages*

Beginning Writer's Answer Book—This book answers 900 of the most often asked questions about every stage of the writing process. You'll find business advice, tax tips, plus new information about online networks, databases and more. *#10394/$17.99/336 pages.*

Voice & Style—Discover how to create character and story voices! You'll learn to write with a spellbinding narrative voice, create original character voices, write dialogue that conveys personality and make the story's voices harmonize into a solid style. *#10452/ $15.99/176 pages.*

Getting the Words Right: How to Rewrite, Edit & Revise—Reduction, rearrangement, rewording and rechecking—the 4 Rs of powerful writing. This book provides concrete instruction with dozens of exercises and pages of samples to help you improve your writing through effective revision. *#10172/$14.99/218 pages/paperback*

Freeing Your Creativity: A Writer's Guide—Discover how to escape the traps that stifle your creativity. You'll tackle techniques for banishing fears and nourishing ideas so you can get your juices flowing again. *#10430/$14.99/176 pages/paperback*